Henry Moore
and the Arts Council Collection

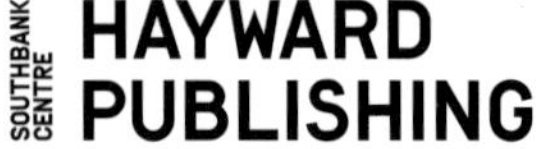

SOUTHBANK CENTRE

HAYWARD PUBLISHING

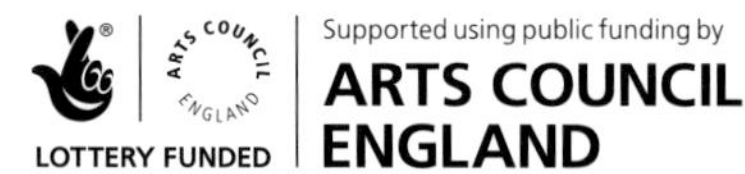

LOTTERY FUNDED

Supported using public funding by

ARTS COUNCIL ENGLAND

henry moore

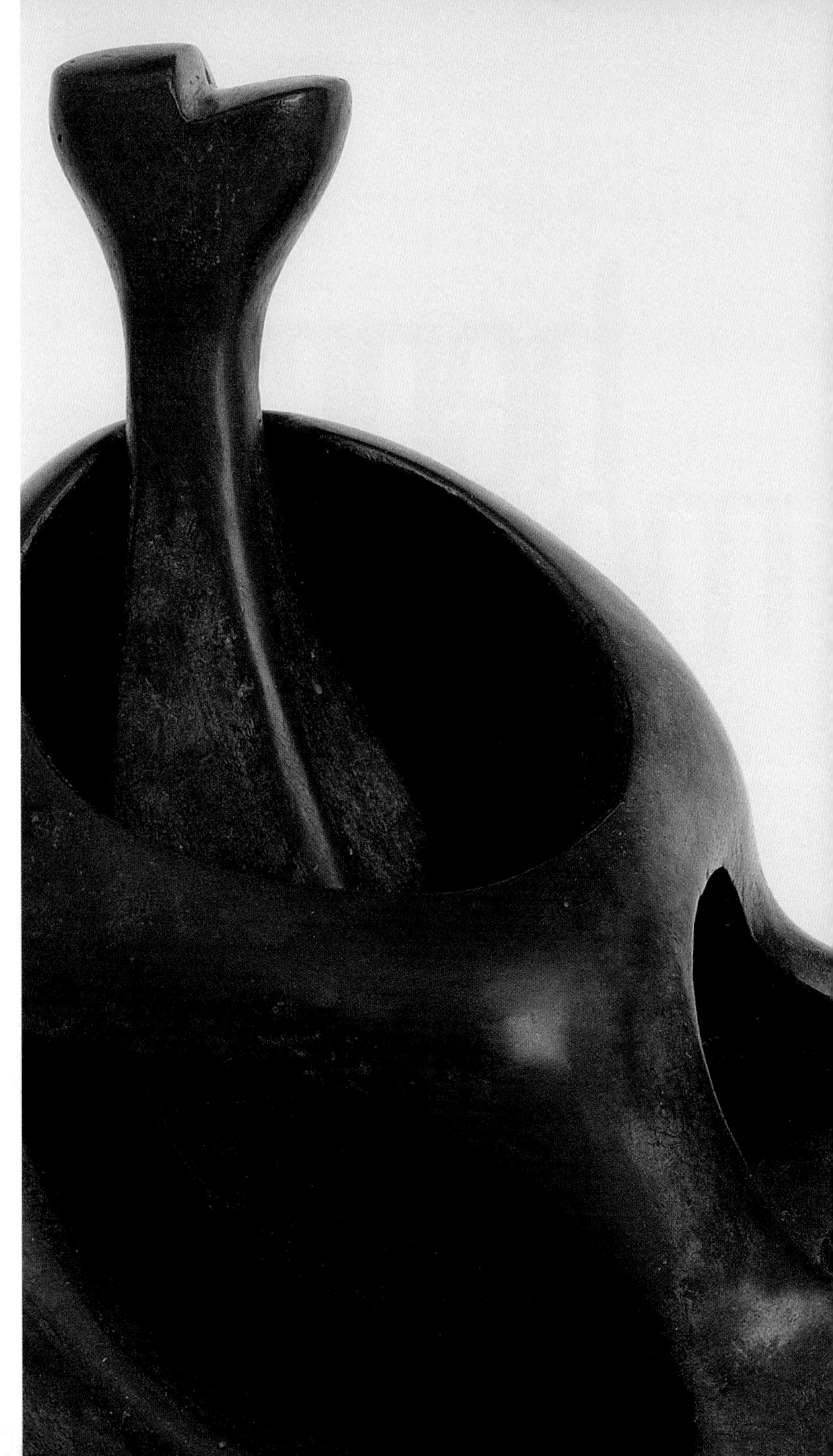

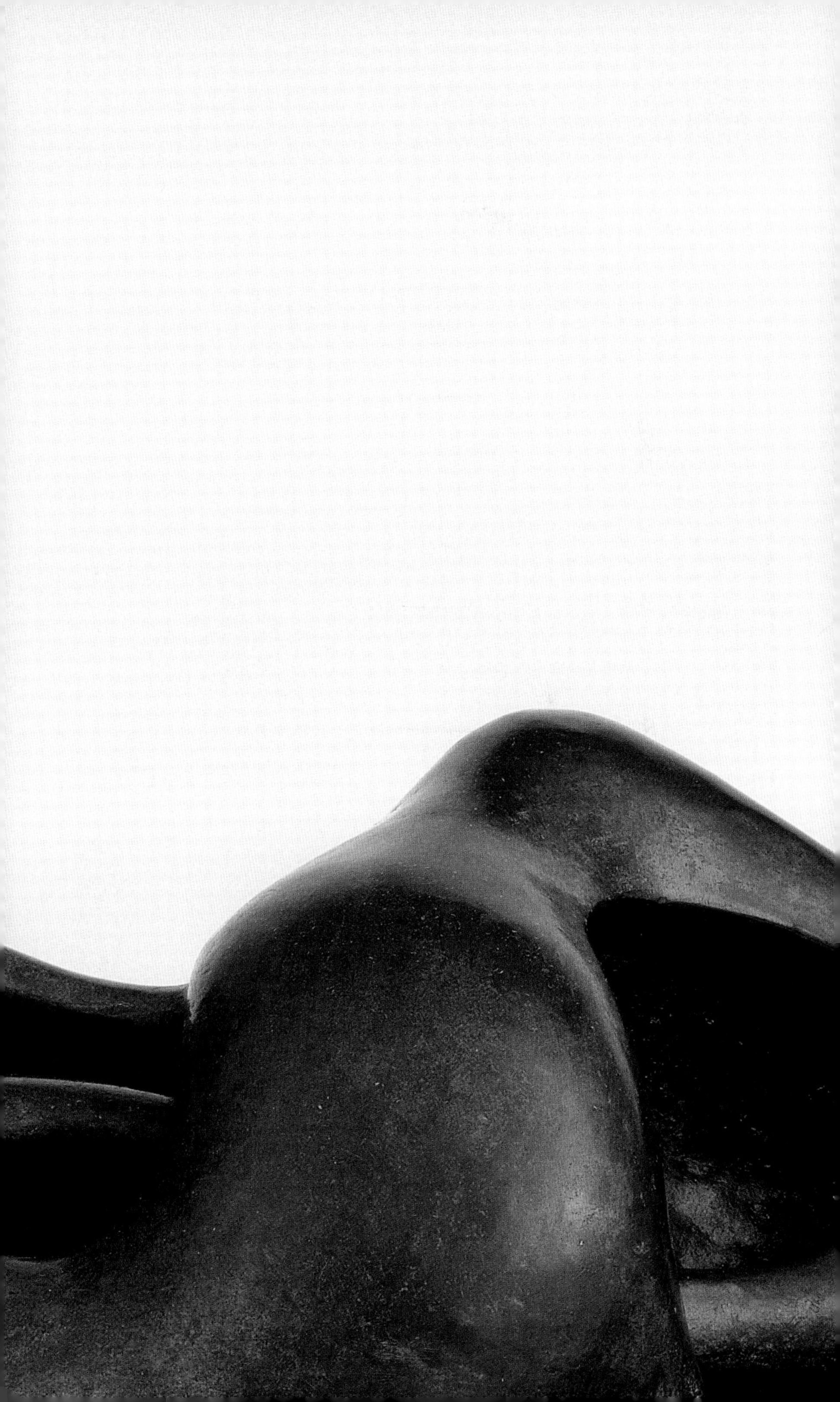

contents

A product of judicious early purchasing and gifts from the artist,
the drawings and sculptures by Henry Moore in the Arts Council
Collection touch upon the key themes in his work from the late
1920s to the mid 60s, as well as distilling the artist's response to
the world he lived in. The earliest work in the group, *Drawing for
Figure in Concrete* of 1929 — a study for the sculpture of the same
year now in the collection of the British Council — betrays the
artist's early interest in a non-Western sculptural tradition, as well
as the influence of his predecessor, Jacob Epstein. A slightly later
bronze, *Composition* of 1934 (cast 1961), introduces the use of
natural forms, bones and pebbles, disposed in a grouping that
reminds the viewer of Moore's early association with the European
Surrealist movement.

As the twentieth century tipped, once again, towards
global war, Moore's *Stringed Figure* of 1938 (cast 1960) translated
the pervading anxiety into (literally) tensioned elements within
his work. Sculptural planes created with strings have a transparency
that prefigures Moore's later work, with its emphasis on internal

and external form. The hollowed out and disassembled body of Moore's
Working Model for Reclining Figure: Internal/External Form of 1951
(cast 1963) presents a far from triumphalist vision in the year of the
Festival of Britain but, instead, and like *Helmet Head No.3* of 1960,
speaks of the vulnerable, fearful and damaged body—of the continuing
terrors of the Cold War and nuclear threat.

Later bronzes in the Collection are working models for the
monumental sculptures for which Moore became best known in later
years—major commissions for public work in London, Washington and
New York. A travelling collection, the Arts Council Collection would not
provide an appropriate home for large-scale work—instead what we have
is a group of works scaled to the artist's hand, which, together with some
beautiful sketches and more finished drawings, give an acute and intimate
insight into Moore's approaches and the development of his ideas.

The process of compiling this publication has provided an
opportunity for some critical research into the Collection's holdings and
I should like to record our gratitude to Laura Robinson and Helen Kaplinsky
for their research and the fascinating archival material this has revealed.
Art historian Benedict Read has contributed an insightful text examining the
circumstances by which works entered the Collection, and Jill Constantine,
Senior Curator for the Collection for many years now, has lead the project
throughout. We extend our heartfelt thanks to them both. While this book
will initially accompany a touring exhibition, it is our intention that it will
be useful long afterwards. For this we are indebted to Nadine Monem
and Faye Robson of Hayward Publishing, for their acuity and judgement in
making it not only a valuable academic resource, but a thing of beauty too;
we also extend our thanks to Niall Sweeney and Nigel Truswell at Pony Ltd
for their elegant, eloquent book design. Finally, we should like to thank the
staff of the Henry Moore Foundation at Perry Green for their support in
the making of the publication, as well as its former Head of Collections
and Exhibitions David Mitchinson, for his long memory.

Caroline Douglas
Head of Arts Council Collection

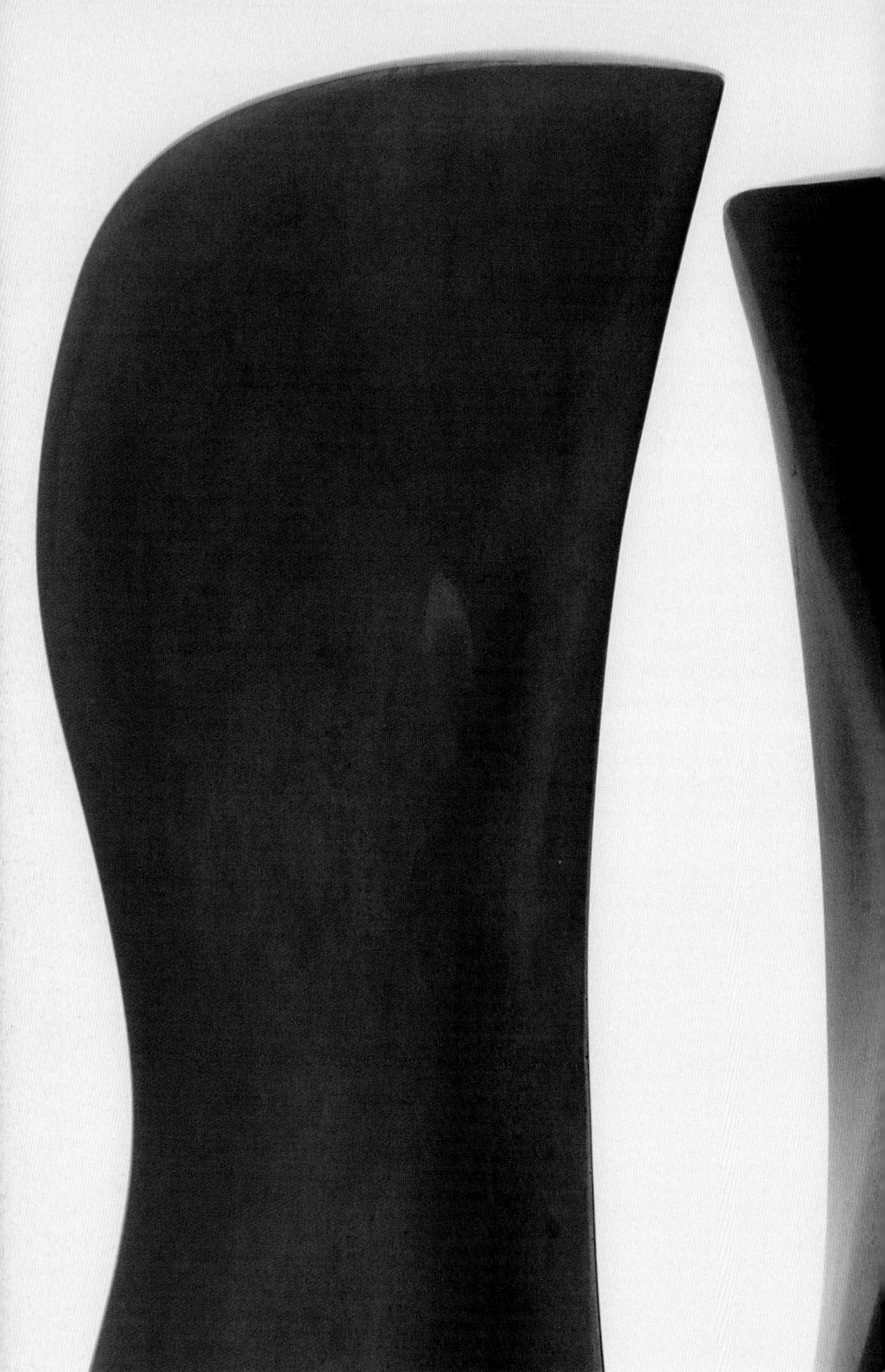

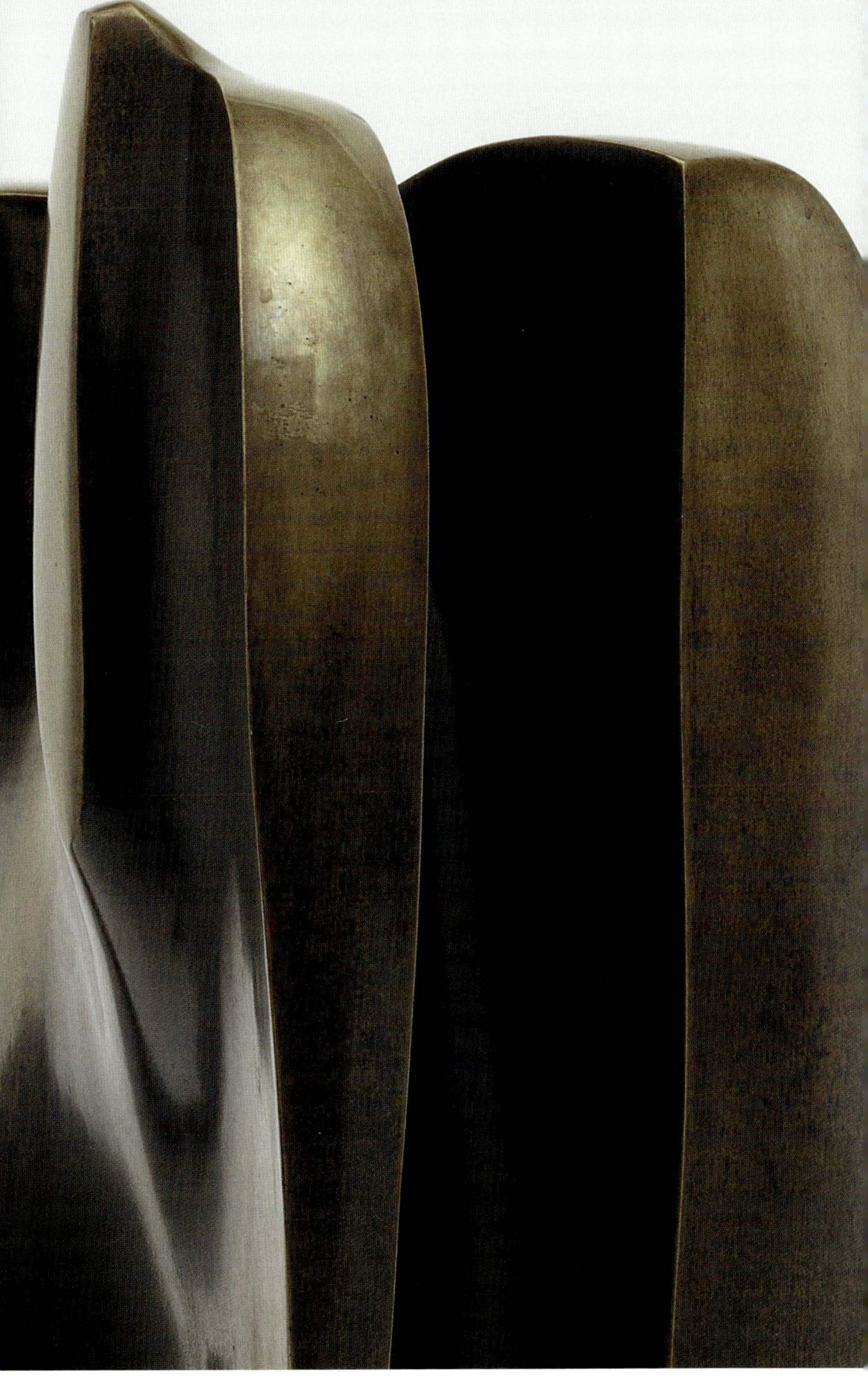

Previous: *Working Model for Knife Edge Two Piece* 1962 (detail).

Henry Moore
and the Arts Council Collection

Henry Moore (right), David Sylvester (centre), Joanna Drew (left) and Monika Kinley (behind), installing Moore's 70th birthday retrospective exhibition, organised by Arts Council of Great Britain at the Tate Gallery, London, July 1968.

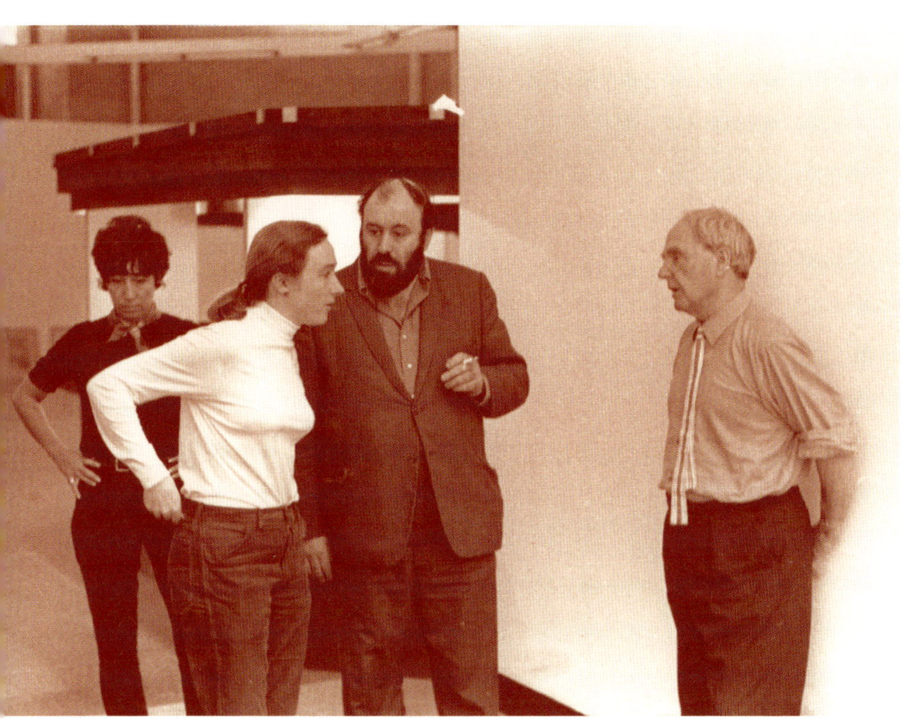

Henry Moore's association with the Arts Council began with its predecessor, the Council for the Encouragement of Music and the Arts (CEMA). In 1942, with money from the London-based charitable fund the Pilgrim Trust, CEMA began to collect works of art by British artists, to be shown up and down the country, often in places where there was no gallery and where original contemporary art had never been seen. In 1946, the Arts Council of Great Britain (ACGB) was created as CEMA's successor and, by December 1978, the Arts Council Collection, as it is now known, had acquired some 5,000 works. Henry Moore was to serve terms on the Art Panel of both institutions between 1942 and 1960, advising them on purchases by other artists for the Collection and himself featuring frequently in exhibitions and public displays that the Council organised.

The Council's acquisition of Moore's work started in 1948 with the drawings *Seated Figure, c.* 1933 (p. 58), and *Women Winding Wool* 1948 (pp. 50–51). In the early years of the Council (and CEMA before it), the selection of acquisitions was made by members of the Art Panel, with input from members of the Council's Art Department.[1] The Panel was a group of art experts who advised the Council; it had a changing membership and regularly, over the years, one can find Moore himself on the Panel, as well as prominent art-world figures, many of whom knew Moore from other contexts. The Directors of Art were Council officers, who directed the operations of their Department, and, again, there is evidence of close friendships between these figures and Moore. There were intermittent acquisitions of Moore's work in the 1950s, but the major purchase came in 1963, when eight sculptures and eight drawings were purchased direct from the sculptor.

Unfortunately, detailed records documenting the machinery of acquisition do not survive, but the Moore purchases that year merited a particular mention in the published Annual Report.[2] We know, for instance, that the Art Panel for 1962–63 included Alan Bowness and David Sylvester. Bowness was a long-time associate of Moore's; he was involved in the publication of the complete catalogue of Moore's sculpture and ultimately became Director of the Henry Moore Foundation. Sylvester had been Moore's secretary briefly after World War II and had published the first serious articles about Moore in *The Burlington Magazine* in 1948. In that year, Moore arranged with the Director of the Art Panel, Philip James, for Sylvester to write the introduction for the touring exhibition *A Retrospective of Drawings by Henry Moore*. Sylvester then went on to curate a crucial series of Arts Council exhibitions on Moore, held in the years 1951, 1955 and 1968. He too was involved in the editing of the complete catalogue of Moore's sculpture.[3] Also on the Panel in the same year were Roland Penrose and R. J. Sainsbury, one-time patrons of Moore, as well as the critic John Russell, a friend of Moore's. The documented sculpture buyers for the Council that year were the sculptor F. E. McWilliam and Alan Bowness—the latter, as mentioned, a close Moore associate—but it would seem that such a major acquisition was a distinct operation managed and arranged executively by the Council's Art Department.

It is important not to forget those who worked for the Department on a full-time basis, especially the Directors of Art. Philip James had joined CEMA in 1941 and became Director of Art in 1942, a post he retained in the Arts Council until 1958, when he was succeeded by Gabriel White. James's association with Moore was extremely close; he wrote the preface to the 1951 exhibition at Tate, *Sculpture and Drawings by Henry Moore*, whose selection he entrusted to Sylvester, and went on to edit a book of Moore's writings and comments, in which the 'most generous expenditure of time and trouble' by Moore and his secretary, Mrs Tinsley, is warmly acknowledged.[4] His successor, Gabriel White (who had been James's Assistant Director from 1945), in his turn, was in correspondence with Moore during the 1963 acquisition campaign, when the eight sculptures and eight drawings were purchased from the artist. Thus, when one of the designated works, the plaster version of *Time/Life Screen: Working Model* 1952 was damaged in transit, it was White who negotiated directly with Moore for a bronze—and therefore less fragile—replacement to feature in the purchase (pp. 44–45).

We know from the Arts Council archives how closely Moore was involved in the selection of his works for the Collection, especially those acquired in 1963. So it is legitimate to speculate that there was a rationale behind the selection and that Moore was eager to see represented different significant treatments of three-dimensional form, as he had developed them through his career. *Composition* 1934 (cast 1961, pp. 36–37) reflects a phase in Moore's career when he was investigating the potential of more abstract forms, though it is still possible to detect a reference back to the archetypal 'Reclining Figure' so characteristic of his *oeuvre*. The *Stringed Figure* of 1938 (cast 1960, pp. 48–49) illustrates the short period when Moore was experimenting, by use of suspended strings, with a different way of implying space: that is, by creating a see-through membrane between solids. The *Working Model for Reclining Figure: Internal/External Form* of 1951 (cast 1963, pp. 22–23) shows how Moore continuously worked on the spatial play possible in one of his standard themes, as does *Helmet Head No. 3* of 1960 (pp. 64–65), which, in turn, relates to *Sculptural Object* 1960 (pp. 26–27). The *Time/Life Screen: Working Model* of 1952 (cast 1964) commemorates a major public work by Moore: the screen attached to the Time-Life building, which overlooks London's Bond Street — a significant instance of Modernist architecture's arrival in post-war London. The *Head of a King* 1952–53 (cast

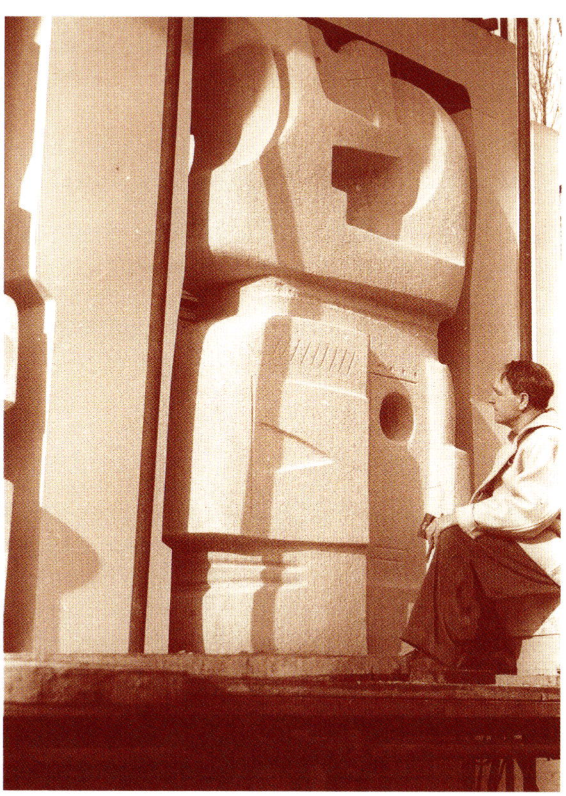

Henry Moore working on *Time/Life Screen* 1952–53 at Perry Green.

15

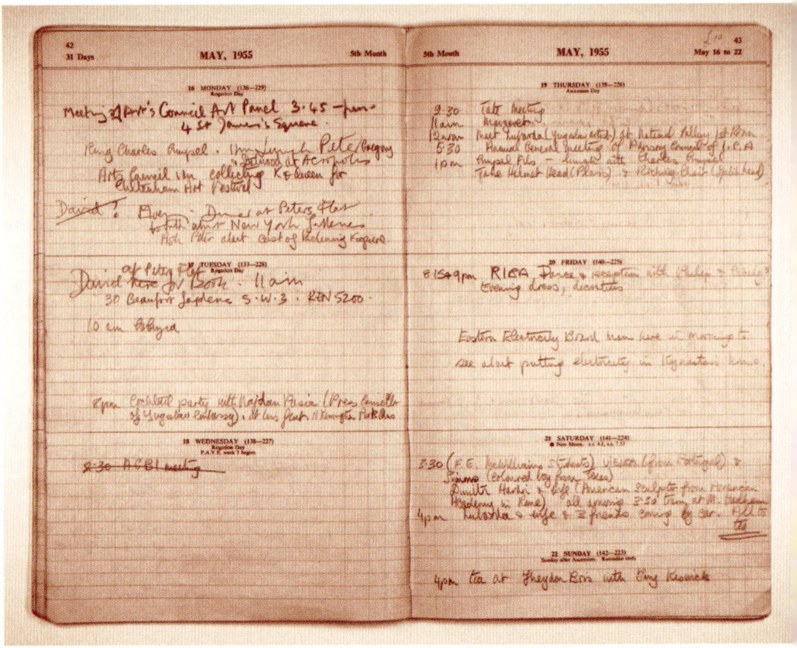

Henry Moore's office diary open to pages 16–22 May 1955.

1962, pp. 40–41) is associated with one of Moore's most iconic sculptures, the *King and Queen* of 1952–53, located in collections around the world. The *Seated Figure against Curved Wall* 1956–57 (pp. 30–33) is a marker for Moore's most prestigious international commission, the *UNESCO Reclining Figure* 1957–58, while *Working Model for Knife Edge Two Piece* 1962 (pp. 52–53) cannot fail to recall, for British audiences, the version placed outside the Houses of Parliament in London, frequently seen on television as a backdrop to political reportage.

The two final Moore works to enter the collection were *Head: Lines* of 1955 (p. 57), bought in 1966 — this was one of a series of studies of bird and animal heads that Moore worked on at the same time as his *Upright Motives* (the most famous of which became known as 'The Glenkiln Cross') — and *Slow Form: Tortoise* of 1962 (pp. 60–61), acquired in 1968 at the suggestion of Sylvester and, like the *Head*, one of a series of concurrently evolving studies relating to larger works.

The range of Moore's drawings in the collection is as significant as that of the sculptures and Moore was emphatic about the importance of drawing for him. *Ideas for West Wind Relief*, c. 1927 (p. 42) marks a crucial breakthrough for Moore in being chosen — along with contemporaries such as Jacob Epstein and Eric Gill — for a very public commission: the sculpture that would become *West Wind* 1928–29 on the London Transport Headquarters at St James's Park Underground station. *Standing Nude*, c. 1929 (p. 55) is a typical figure study of this period, as is *Drawing for Figure in Concrete* of the same year (p. 25). A group of studies from 1932, including *Ideas for Sculpture* (p. 34) and *Ideas for Sculpture: Transformation of Bones* (pp. 38–39) are very much ideas-in-progress for sculpture, sometimes mutating the natural shapes of bones towards potential sculptures, just as *Ideas for Stone Carving c. 1934* (p. 62) does with stones — Moore is known to have taken inspiration from the pebble forms found on Happisburgh beach in Norfolk, where he holidayed in 1931. The *Seated Figure* (p. 58) drawing of *c.* 1933 is a reversion to the typical figure study, while *Studies of the Artist's Child* 1946 (p. 66) refers to his daughter Mary, born that year. *Women Winding Wool* 1948 refers to a practice only too common in the years of post-World War II austerity.

The drawings are, of course, 'one-offs'; each one is original and unique and bears, if you like, the artist's own thumb-print. The bronzes though are different. As it turns out, each one of the Council's bronzes post-date the work's initial version. *Composition* 1934 is a bronze cast of 1961, the *Stringed Figure* a 1960 cast after the original of 1938; *Working Model for Reclining Figure: Internal/External Form* and *Time/Life Screen: Working Model* were both cast specially for the Arts Council in 1963, *Head of a King* was a unique cast for the Arts Council in 1962, after the full-length bronze *King and Queen* of 1952–53. 919 individual sculptures are listed in the Moore sculpture *Complete Catalogue*, but this figure is a little misleading.[5] If we read between the lines, we learn that Moore in fact made numerous original copies of these works, in editions, usually in bronze. The Council's *Seated Figure against Curved Wall* 1956–57, for example, relates to Moore's major commission the *UNESCO Reclining Figure* 1957–58, the original, unique marble of which is at UNESCO headquarters in Paris. In the build-up towards this work, Moore worked on ideas in three dimensions, often at quite small scale. Originally in clay, these themes and variations were later cast in bronze. Of the 22 distinct works so evolved (like the ACC's *Seated Figure*), Moore produced no less than 261 bronze casts, 32 of which were over five feet high.

There are issues arising from this scale of production, particularly the question of 'originality'. If one is a hard line 'Truth to Material' believer, somehow Moore's experimentation with multiple media within his editions seems a betrayal; the artist, we feel, has an obligation to somehow respect the unique demands of the medium he is working in. But such notions, critically widely voiced since the end of the nineteenth century, can be aligned too closely in sculpture with the idea of 'Direct Carving', that is, the artist hacking out from stone or wood a unique work of art. It is equally possible that working in clay or bronze has its own set of truths. Moore was quite clear that working in clay had its distinct rules: 'I like clay, it's wonderful stuff to punch and feel that the imprint of your fist is left in it'. Moore was also clear about the procedures involved in producing work in bronze. Normally a plaster version is prepared, from which a mould can be made, into which, eventually, the bronze is poured. 'I prepare my plasters for bronzes with a mixture of modelling and carving… I don't think it matters how a thing is produced… what counts really is the vision it expresses… it's the quality of the mind revealed behind it, rather than the way it's done.'[6] It is, Moore asserts, the vision that counts, so that however much technical and practical assistance the artist receives from others—and Moore had an enviable record of employing assistants who later expressed their gratitude to him for providing the basic experience of how to produce sculpture, including artists such as Anthony Caro and Philip King—the originating artist ensures that the final product matches his intention.

It was, of course, useful for the Arts Council that Moore was able and willing to provide works in editions and that he had, in the post-war period, specialised in making his work available at a size that would lend itself to touring around smaller-scale venues. The Arts Council's collection of Moore's sculptures was, in a way, tailor-made for the Council's core agenda of touring works of art. Large-scale sculpture in stone or marble is immensely heavy and expensive to transport, whereas small-scale bronzes, which Moore was willing to produce, fitted the Council's requirements exactly. In addition, we know that Moore went out of his way to ensure that the prices the Arts Council paid, for instance for the 1963 acquisitions, were below market rate.

The Collection is without any doubt a tribute also to Moore's professionalism; he was not a Romantic artist devoted only to 'his muse', but a professional sculptor whose business it was to earn a living; he had worked extremely hard throughout his career as a professional artist, developing means of making his work visible, in such a way that he could support himself through his art. He was also a generous man, as evidenced by the favourable prices he charged the Arts Council, and, through his wealth, he was to create the Henry Moore Foundation, through which subsequently the public have so greatly benefited.

Benedict Read FSA
Senior Visiting Research Fellow
School of Fine Art, University of Leeds

Acknowledgements:
I am extremely grateful to Alan Bowness for crucial advice on the
subject, also to current members of the Arts Council Collection staff
for their assistance with archival material.

1.   See Philip James, introduction to *Paintings, drawings and
     sculpture: A selection from the Arts Council collection*,
     exh. cat., Arts Council of Great Britain, London, 1955,
     unpaginated; Isobel Johnstone, 'Foreword', in *Arts Council
     Collection—A Concise, Illustrated Catalogue*, Arts Council of
     Great Britain, London, 1979, pp. 7–12.
2.   See *Ends and Means: The 18th Annual Report of the Arts
     Council Of Great Britain 1962/63*, Arts Council of Great
     Britain, London, 1963, p. 4.
3.   Sylvester edited the reissue of vol.1 of *Henry Moore—
     Complete Sculpture*. Bowness was the editor of vols 2 to 6
     in the series. These appeared from 1944 onwards and are
     often referred to by scholars as 'LH', the initials of the
     original publishers, Lund Humphries.
4.   Philip James (ed.), *Henry Moore on sculpture: A collection of
     the sculptor's writings and spoken words*, MacDonald,
     London, 1966, p. 5.
5.   See 3.
6.   James, *op. cit.*, see 4, 136.

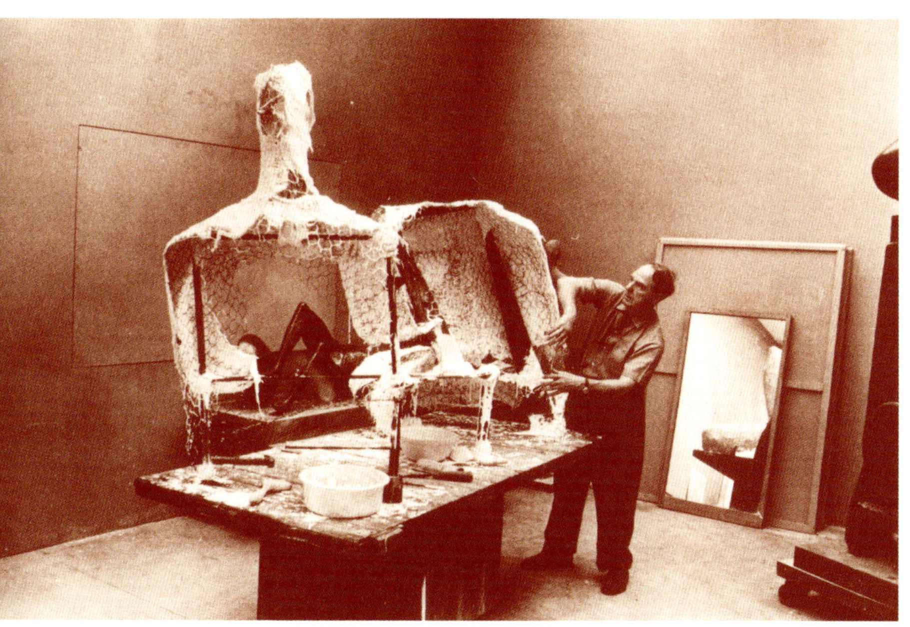

Henry Moore working on the armature for *Working Model for
UNESCO Reclining Figure 1957*, Perry Green.

plates

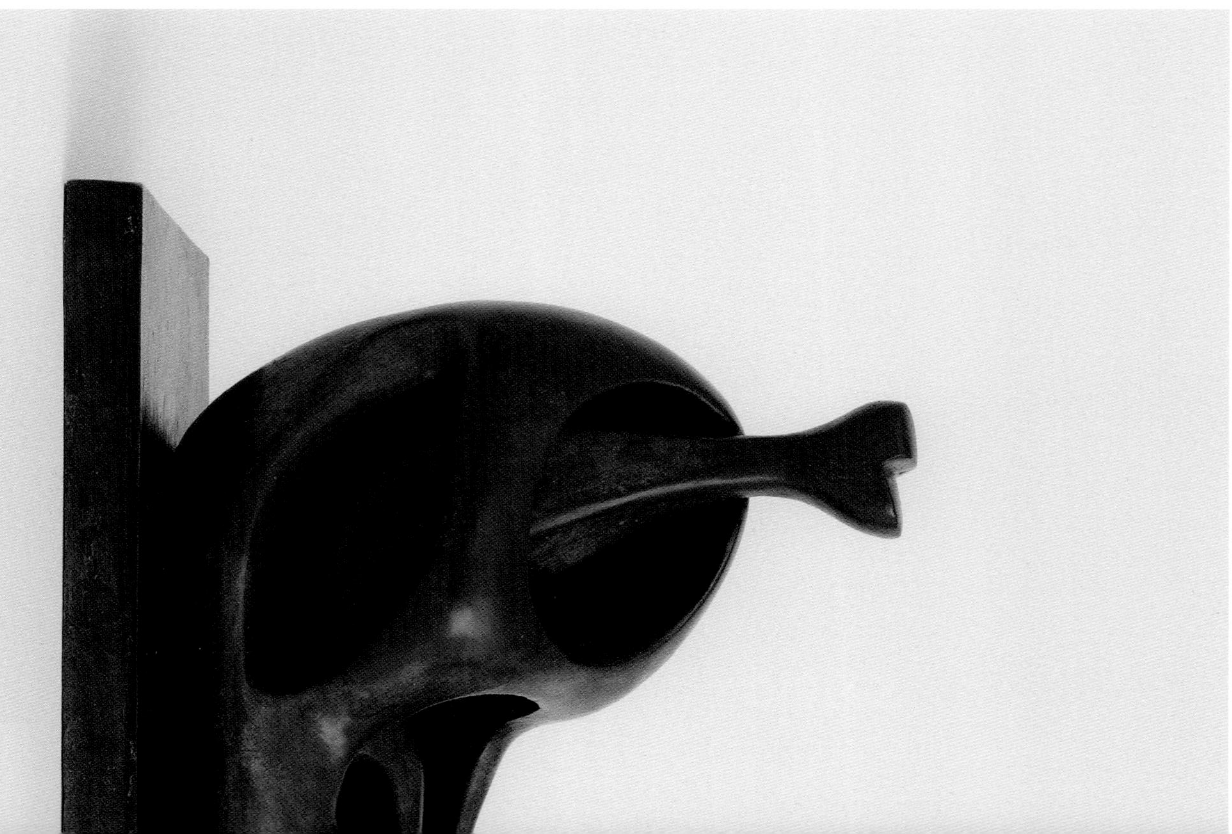

Working Model for Reclining Figure: Internal/External Form 1951, cast 1963

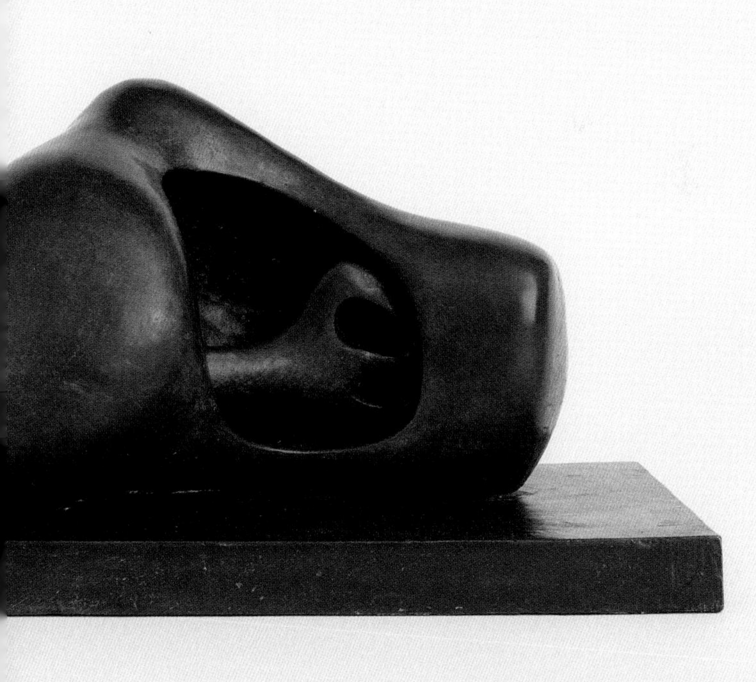

Drawing for Figure in Concrete 1929

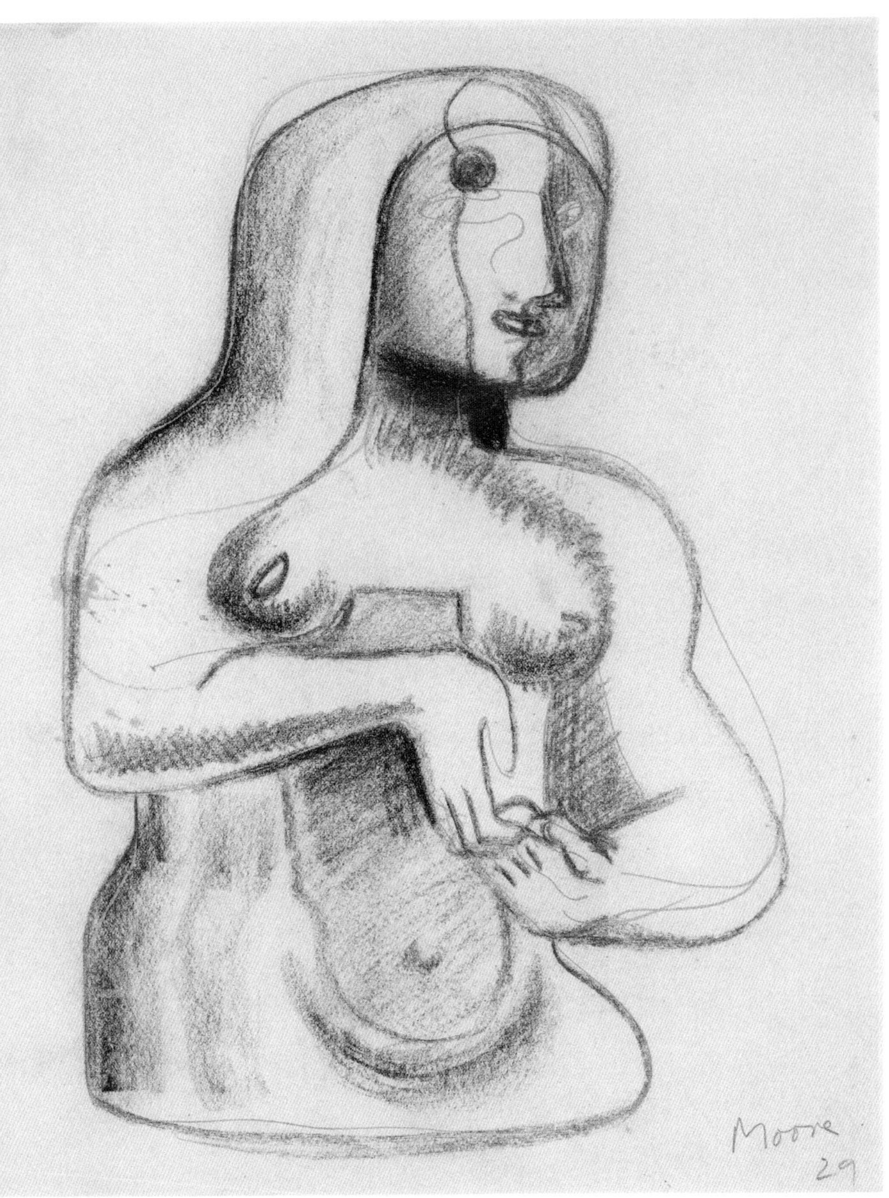

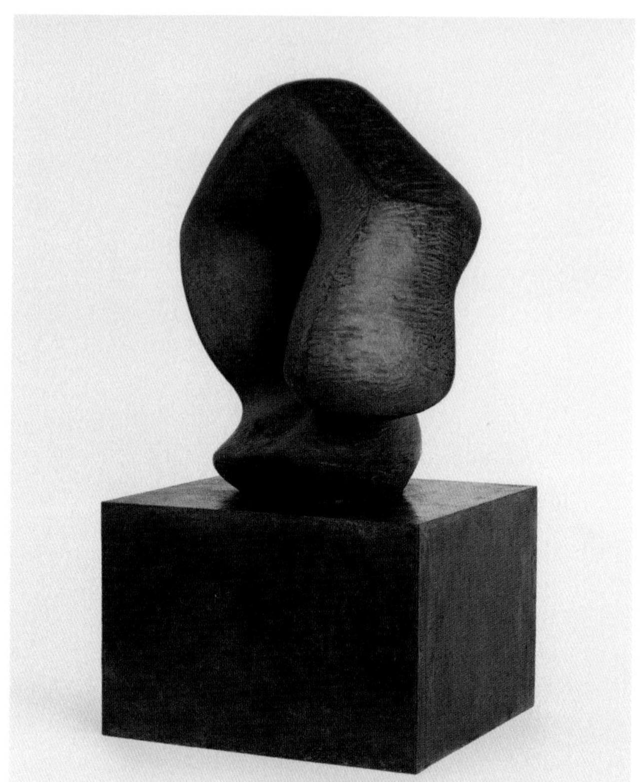

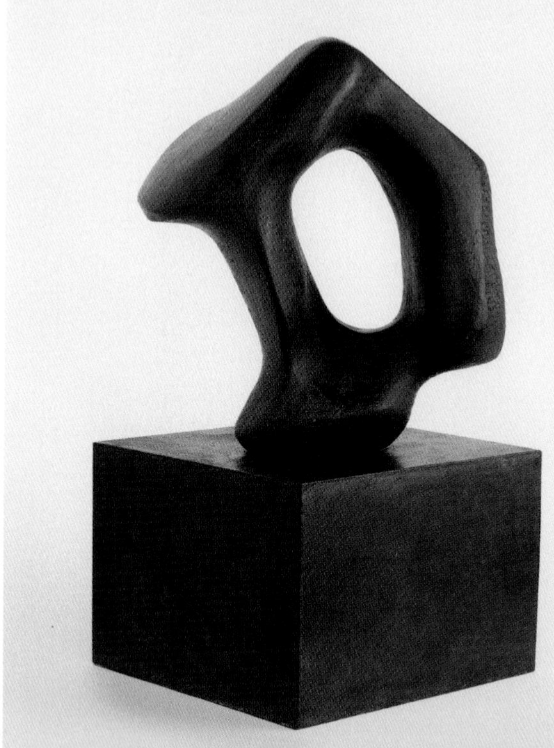

26

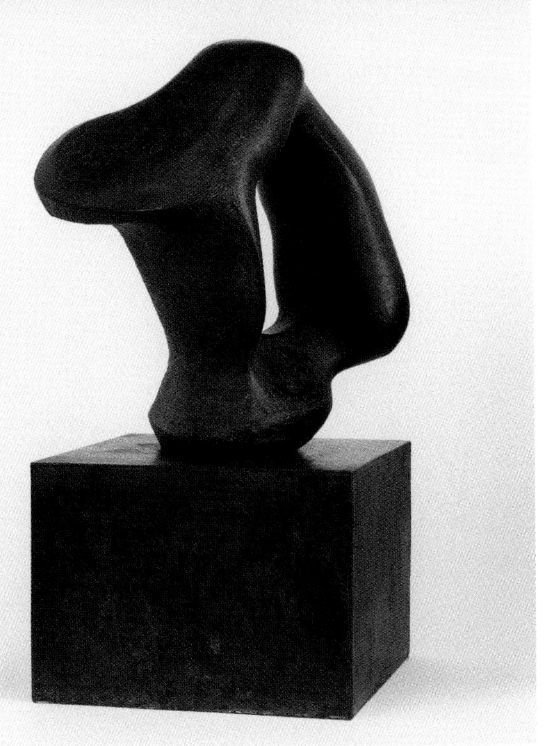

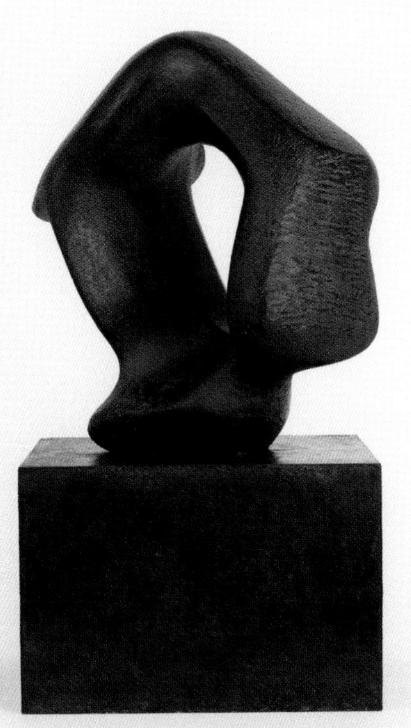

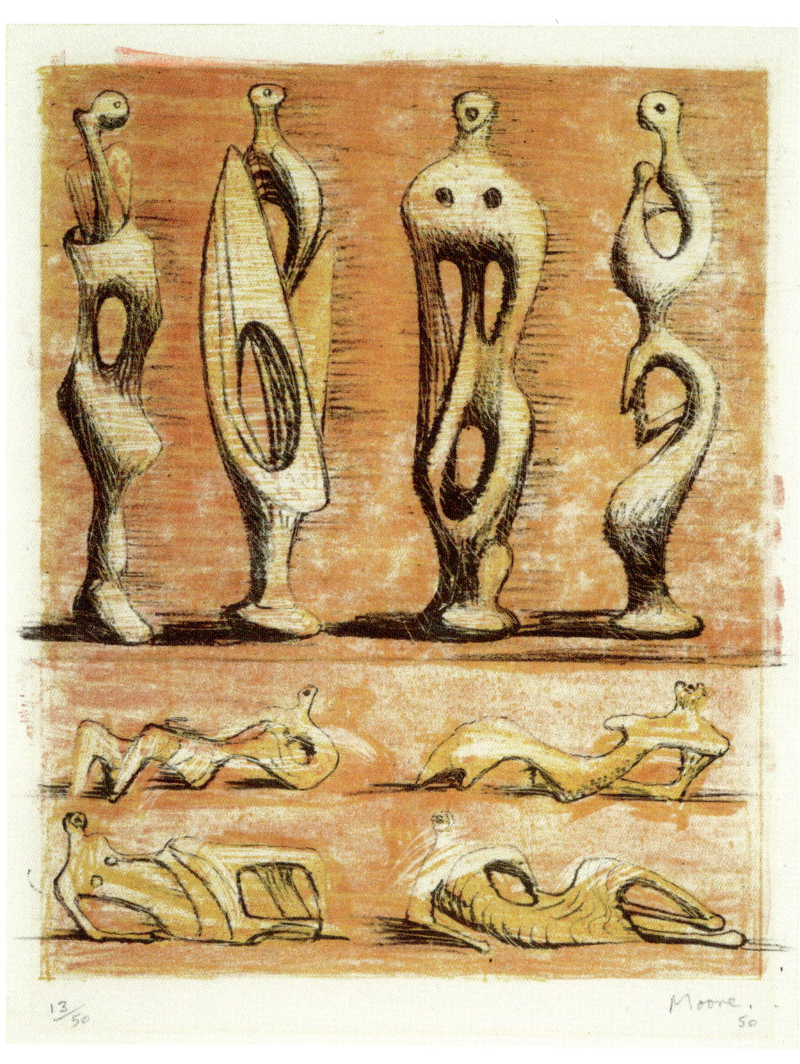

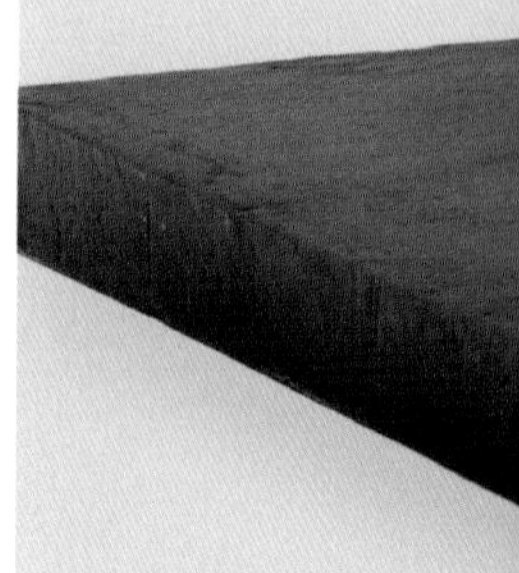

Opposite and overleaf: *Seated Figure against Curved Wall* 1956–57 (details)

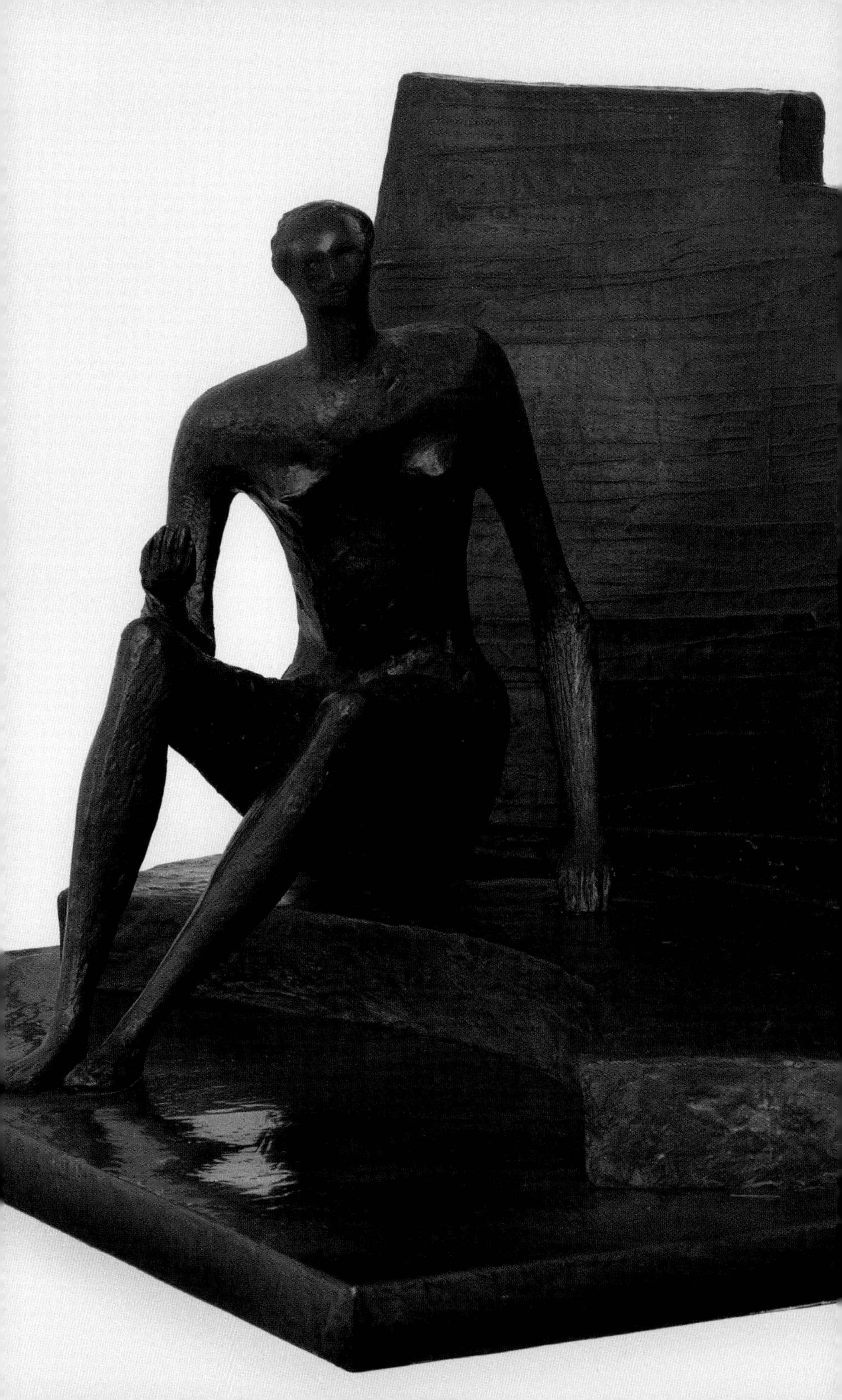

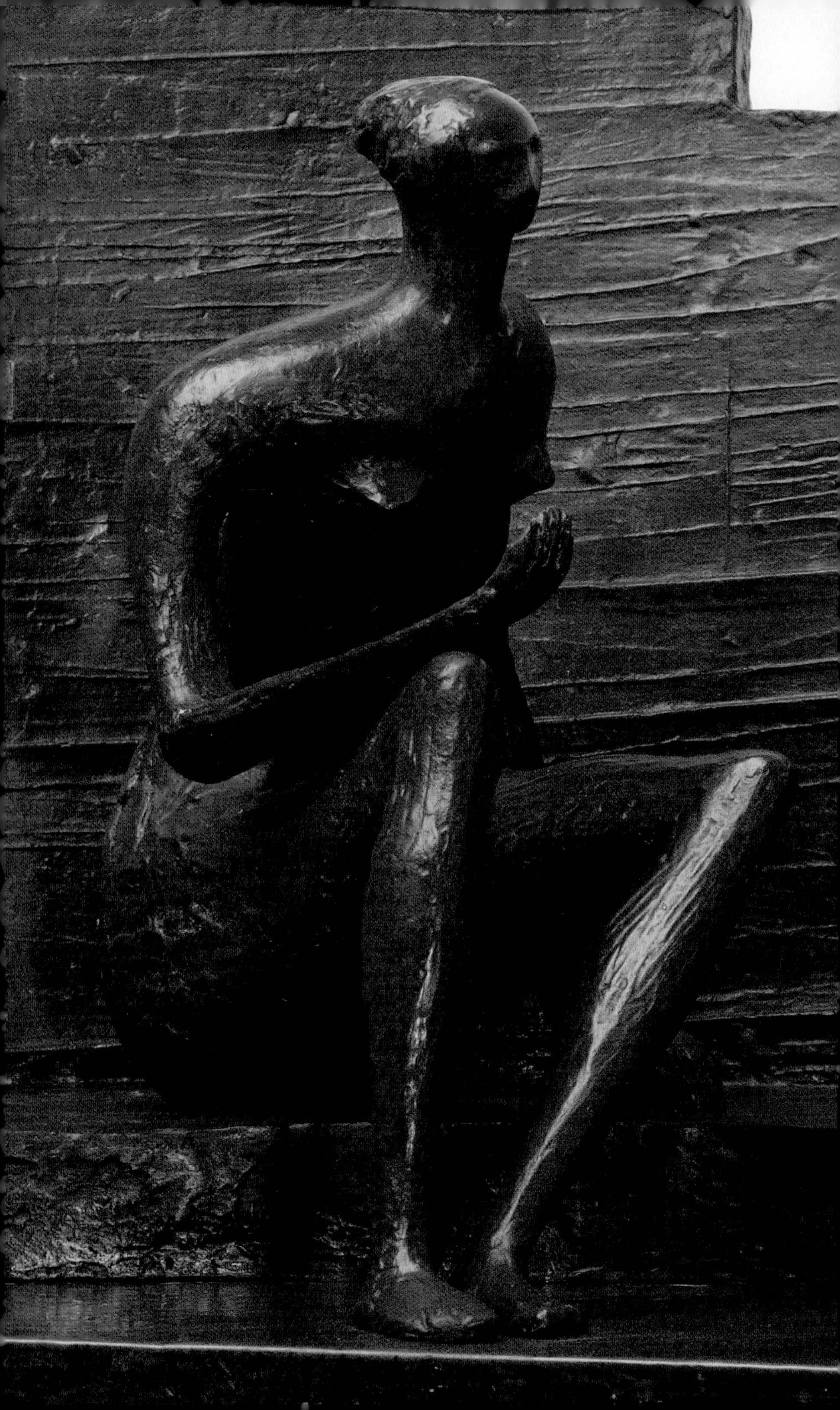

Ideas for Sculpture 1932

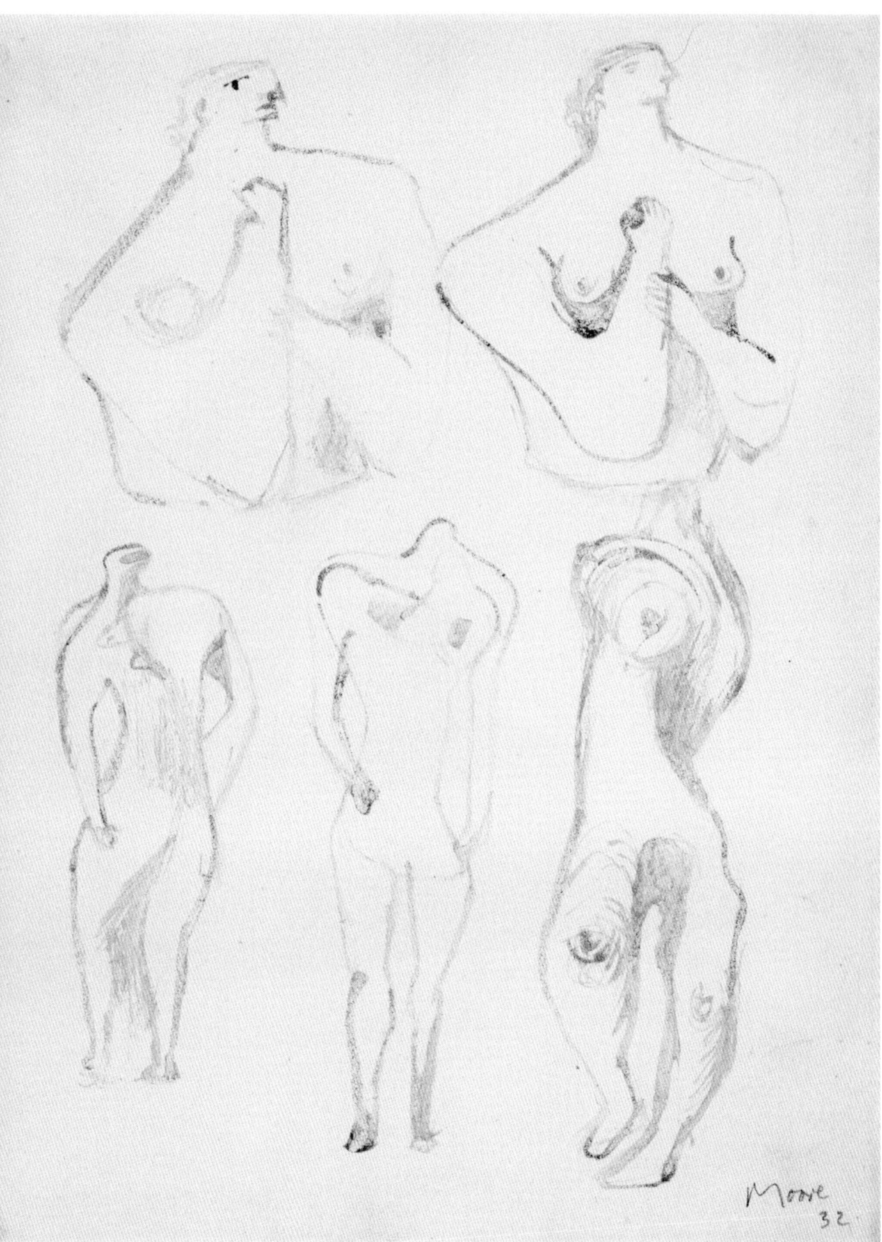
Moore
32

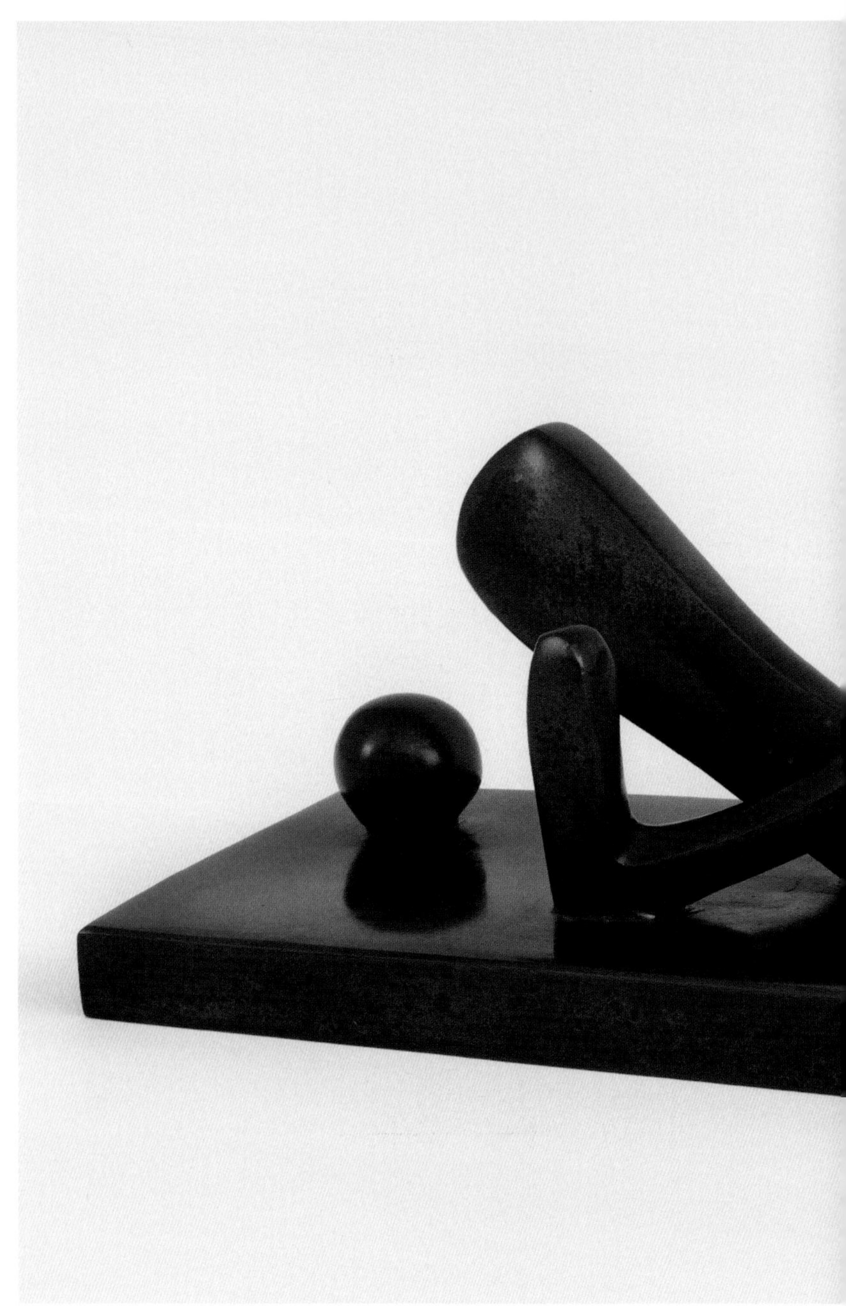

Composition 1934, cast 1961

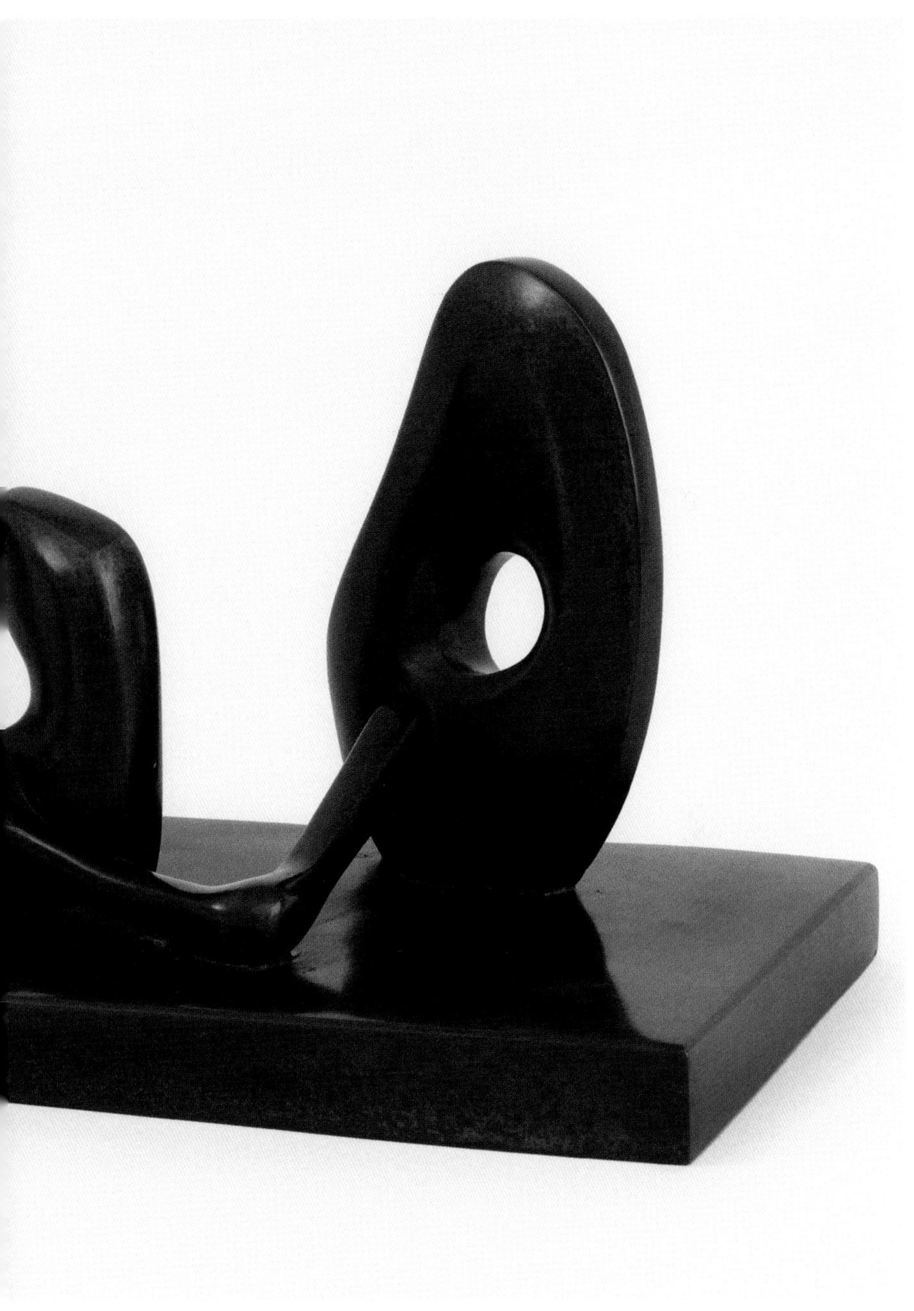

Ideas for Sculpture: Transformation of Bones 1932

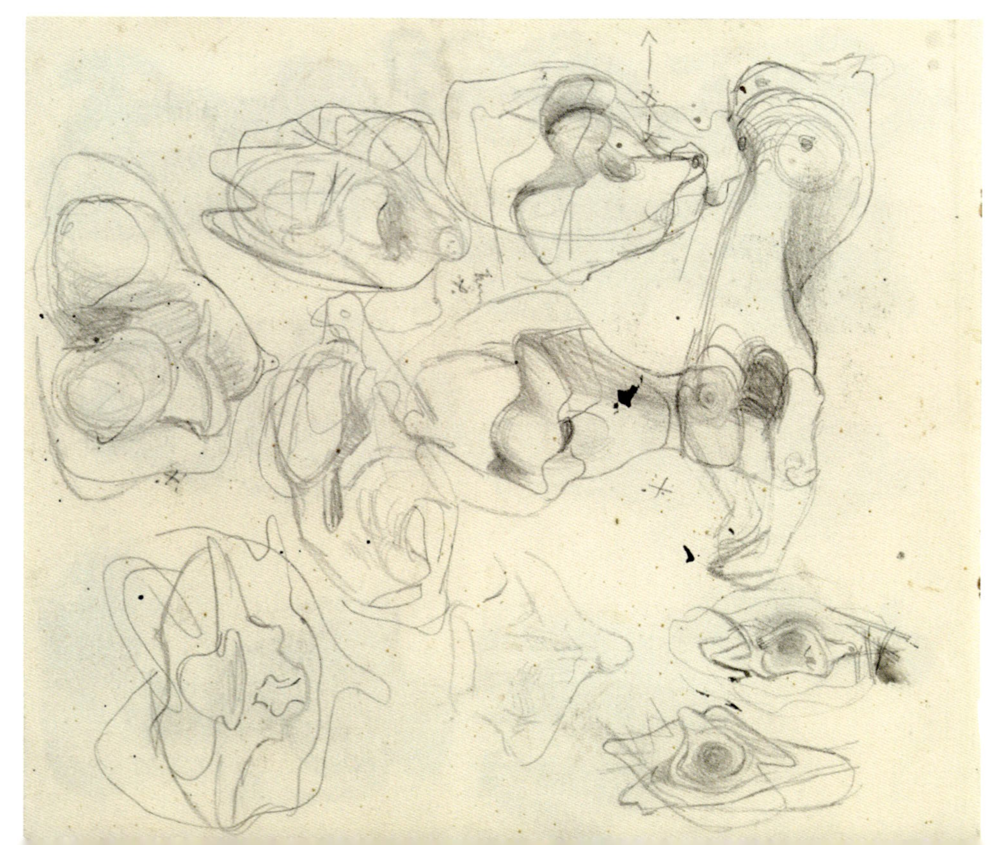

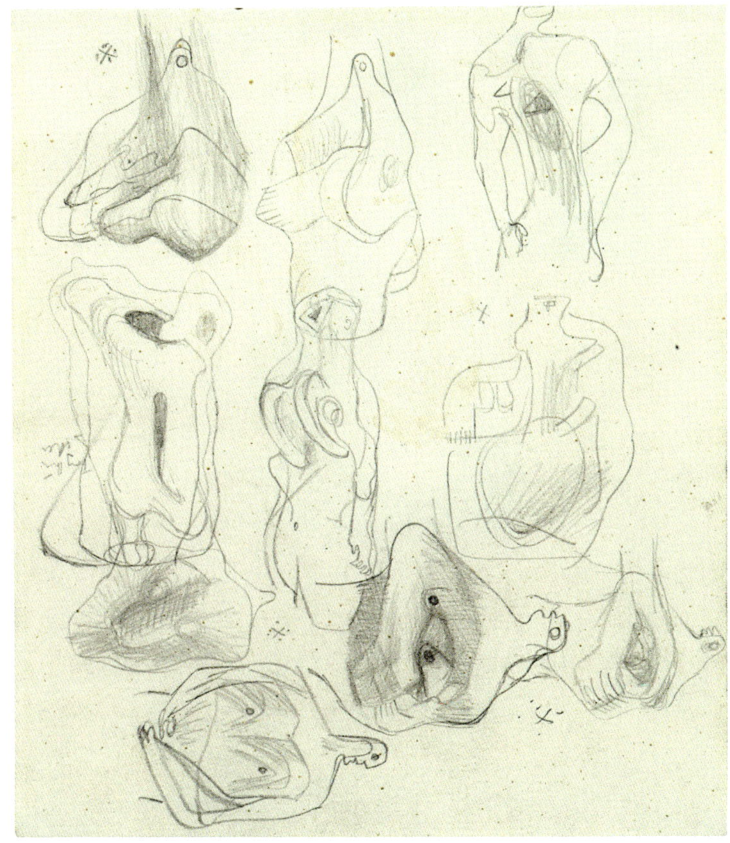

Ideas for Sculpture: Transformation of Bones 1932

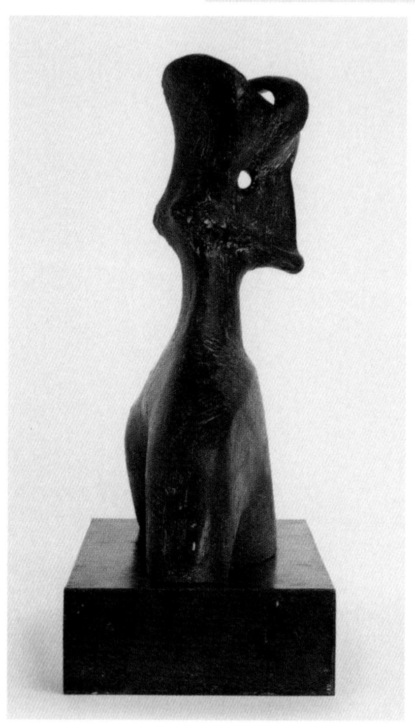

40

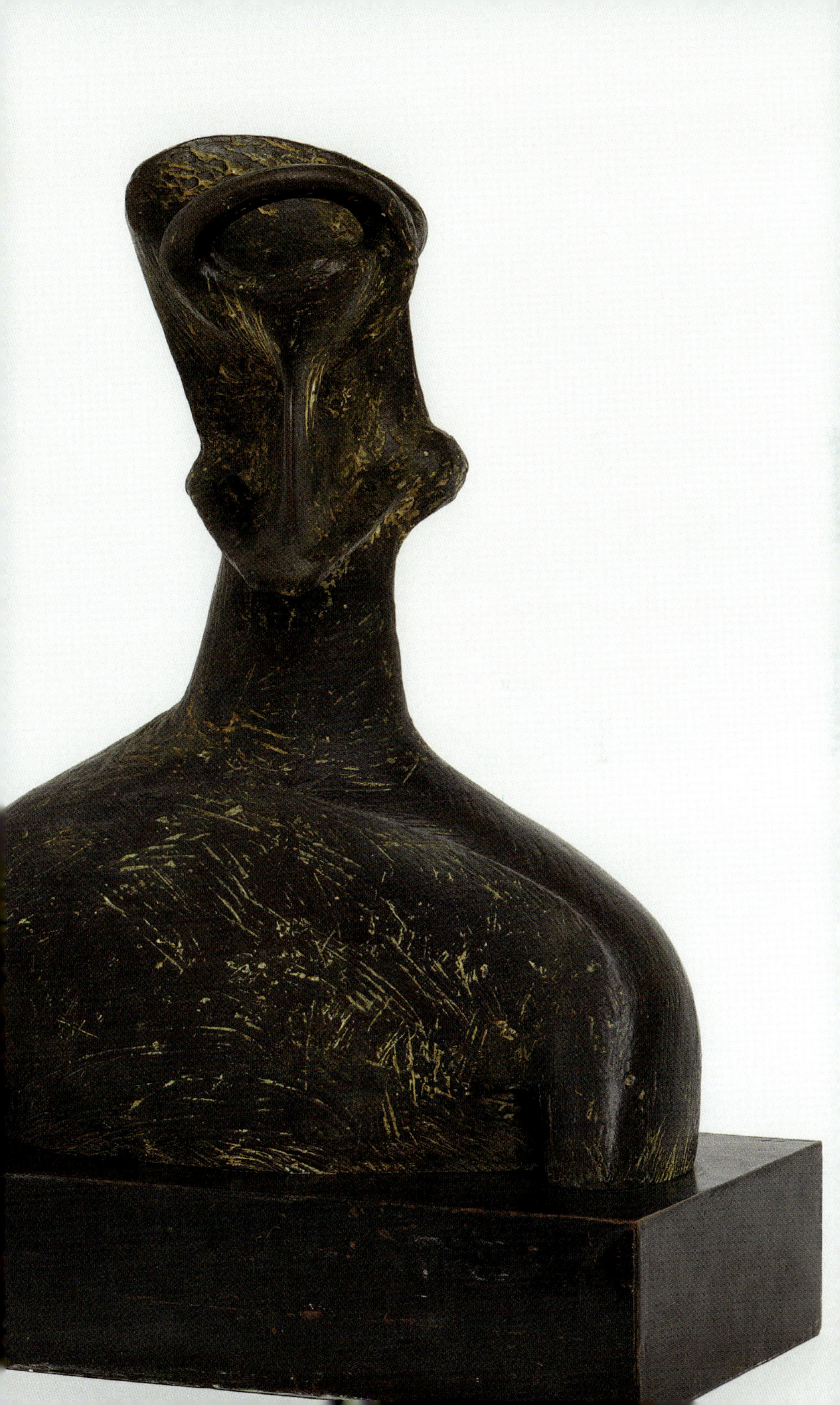

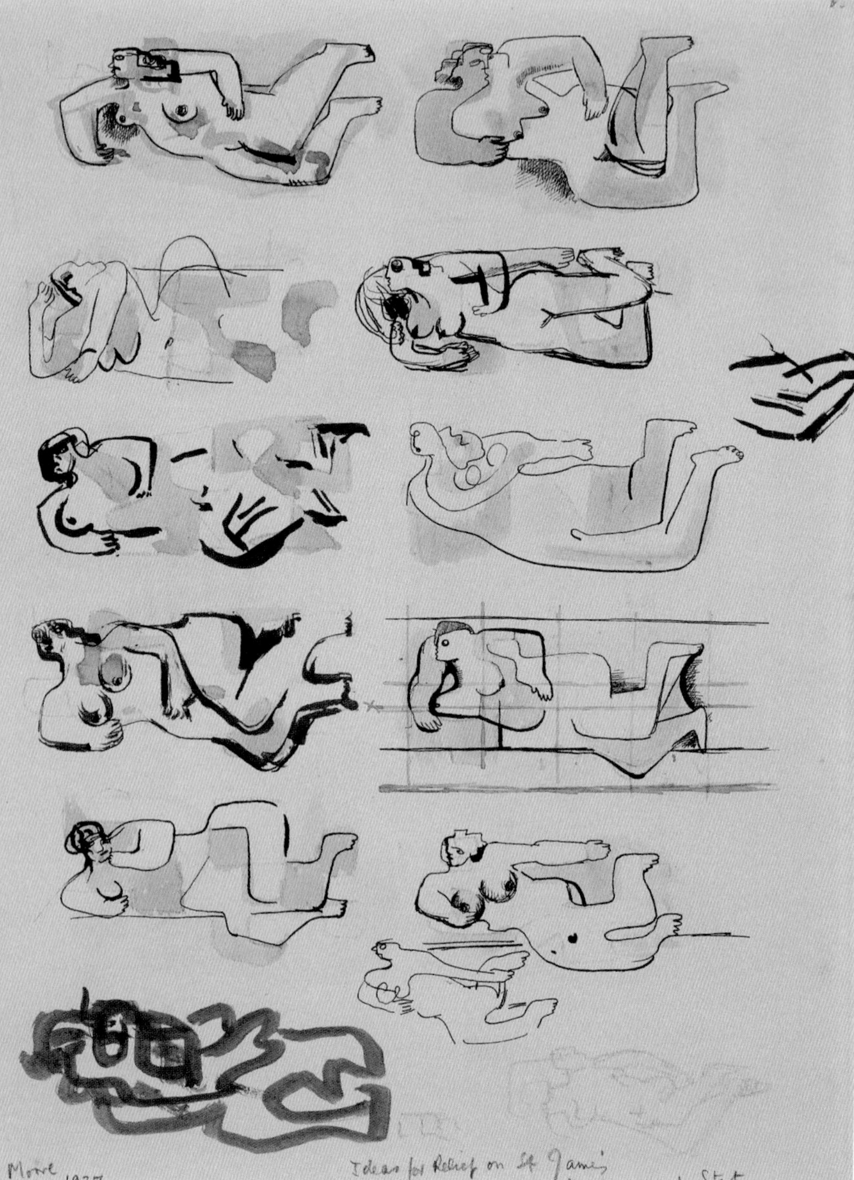

Moore 1927
Ideas for Relief on St James's
Underground Station

Ideas for West Wind Relief, c. 1927

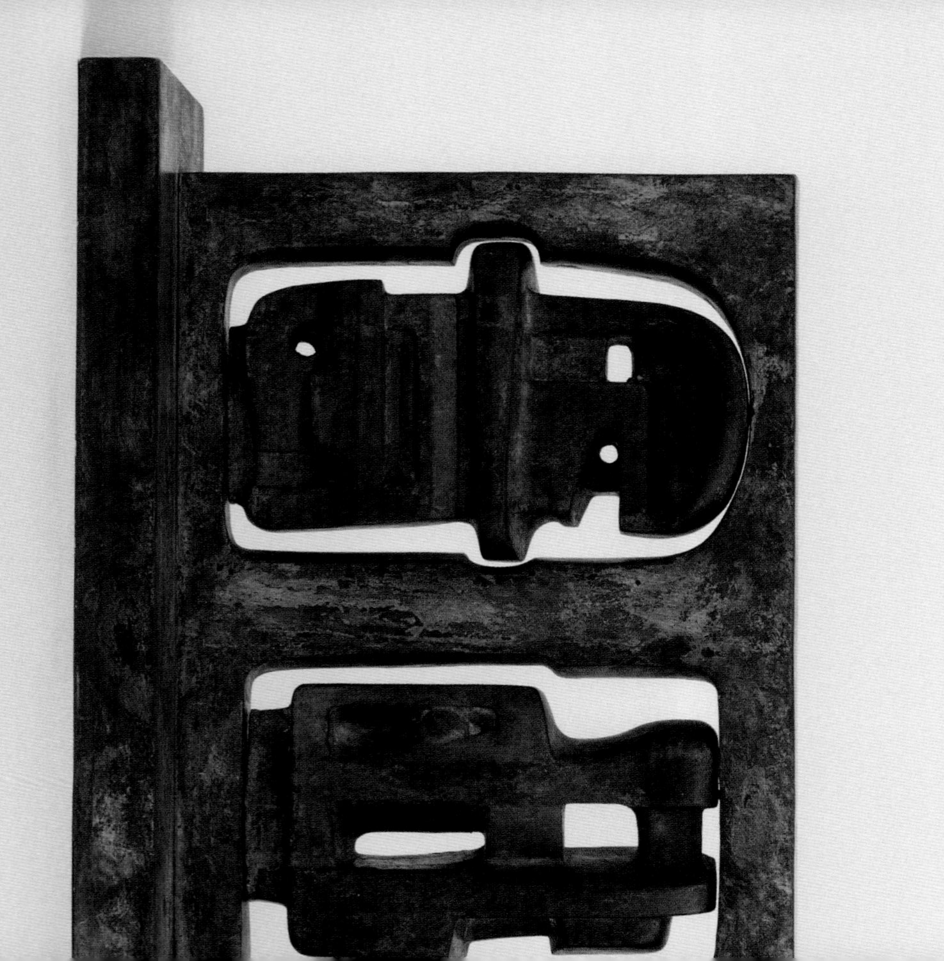

Time/Life Screen: Working Model 1952, cast 1964

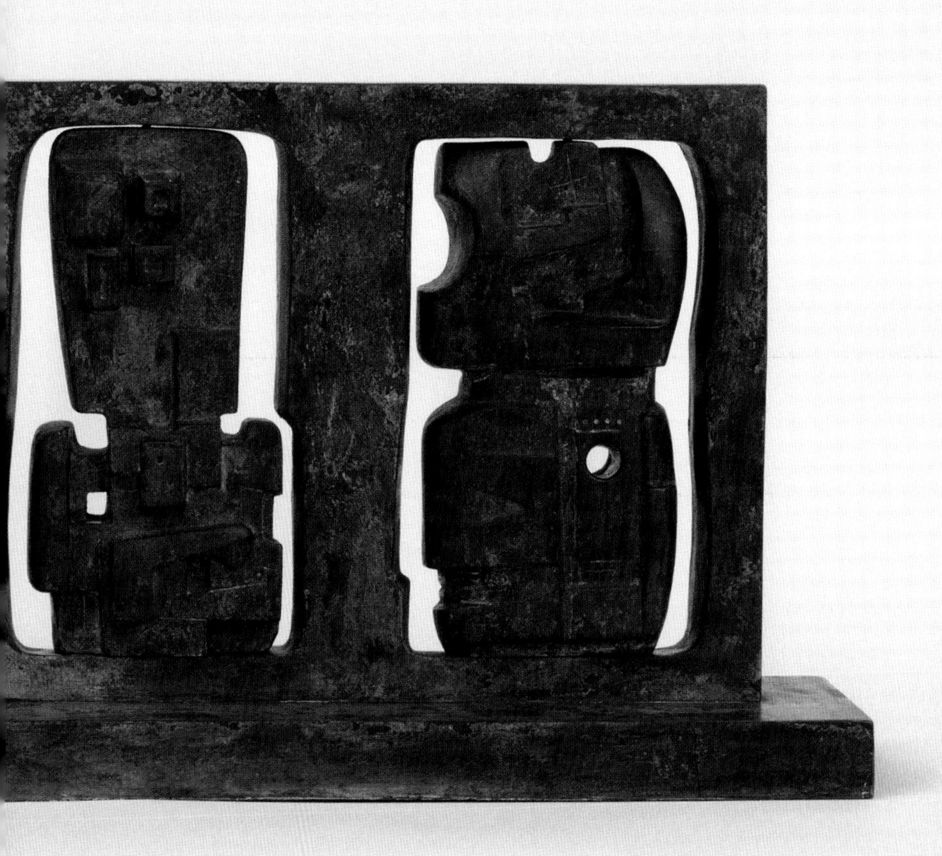

Studies of Bones, Shell and Mushroom 1932

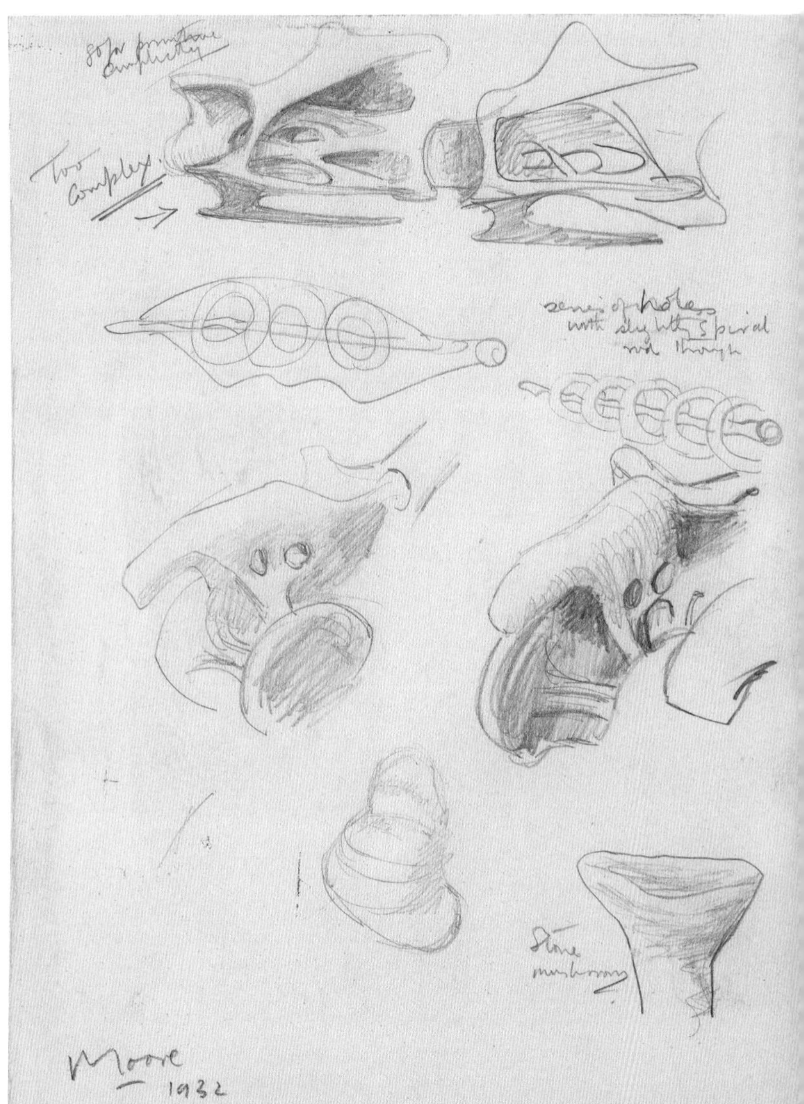

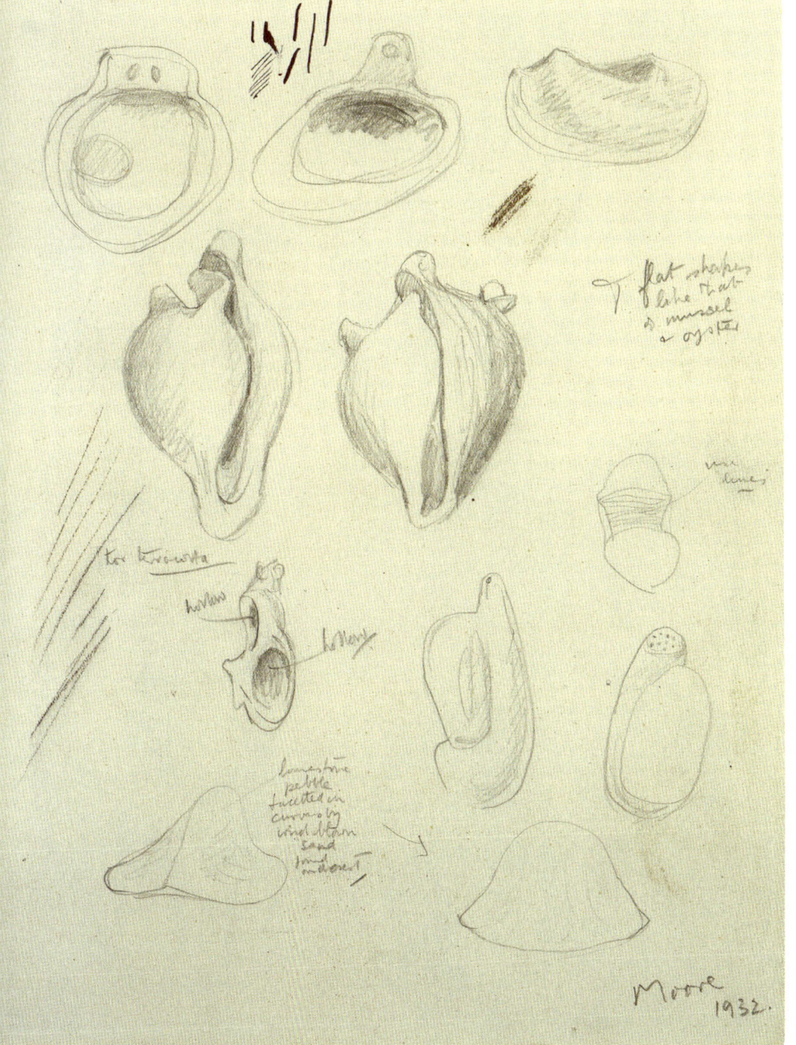

flat shapes
like that
of mussel
& oyster

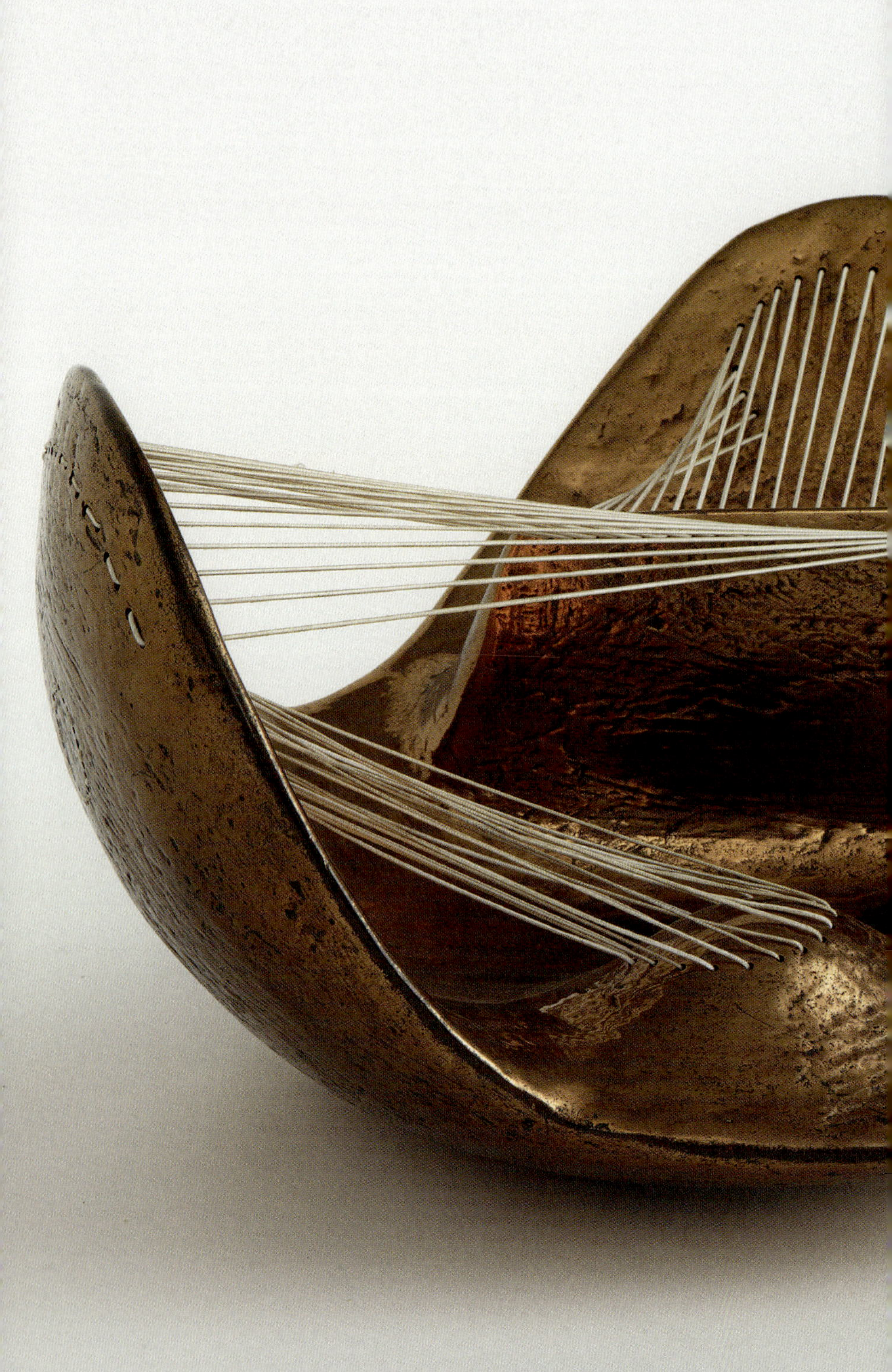

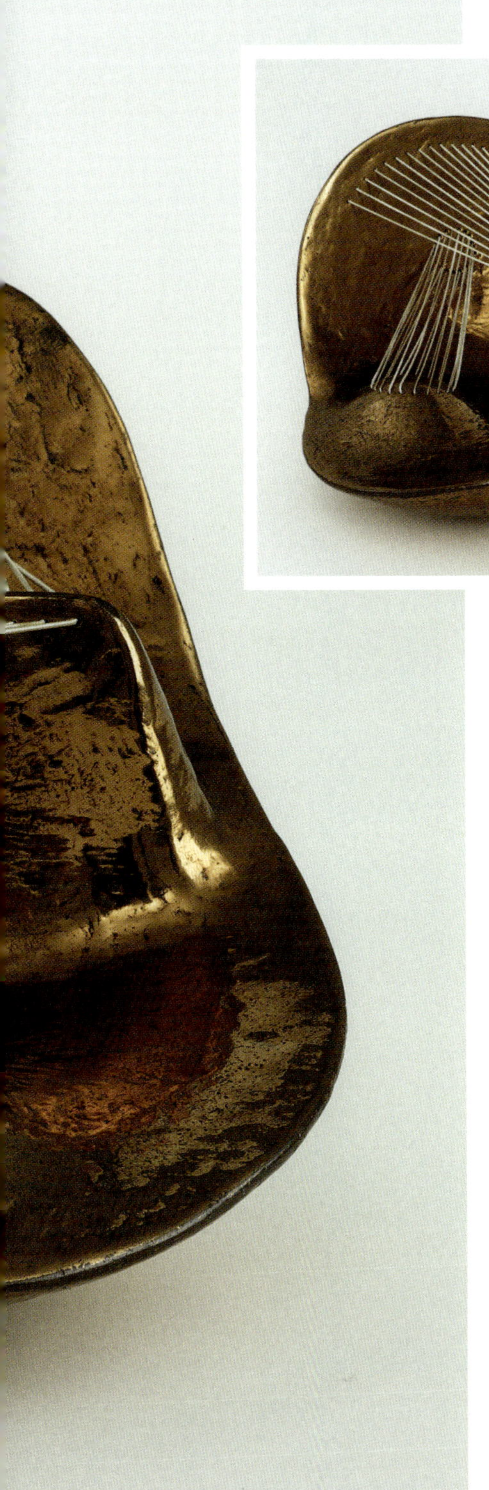

Stringed Figure 1938, cast 1960

49

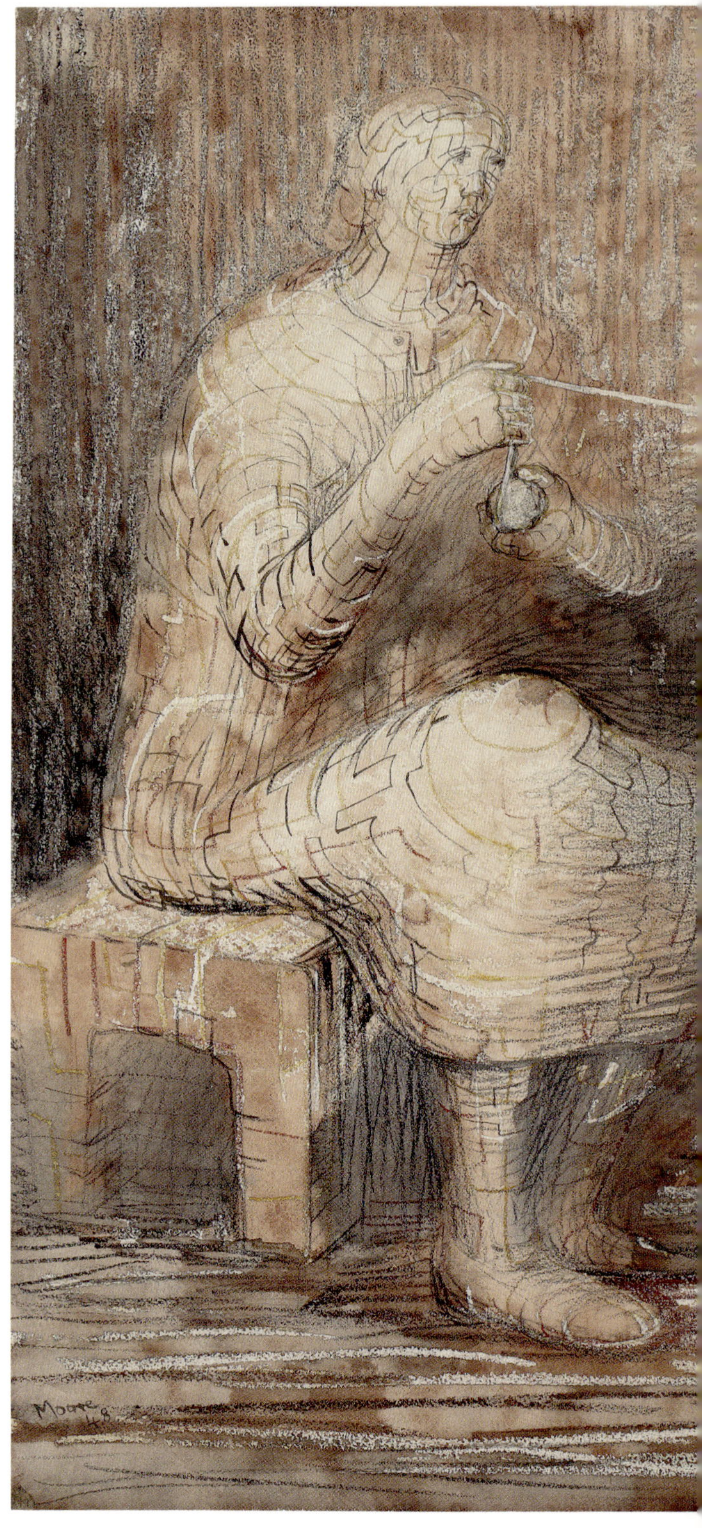

Women Winding Wool 1948

50

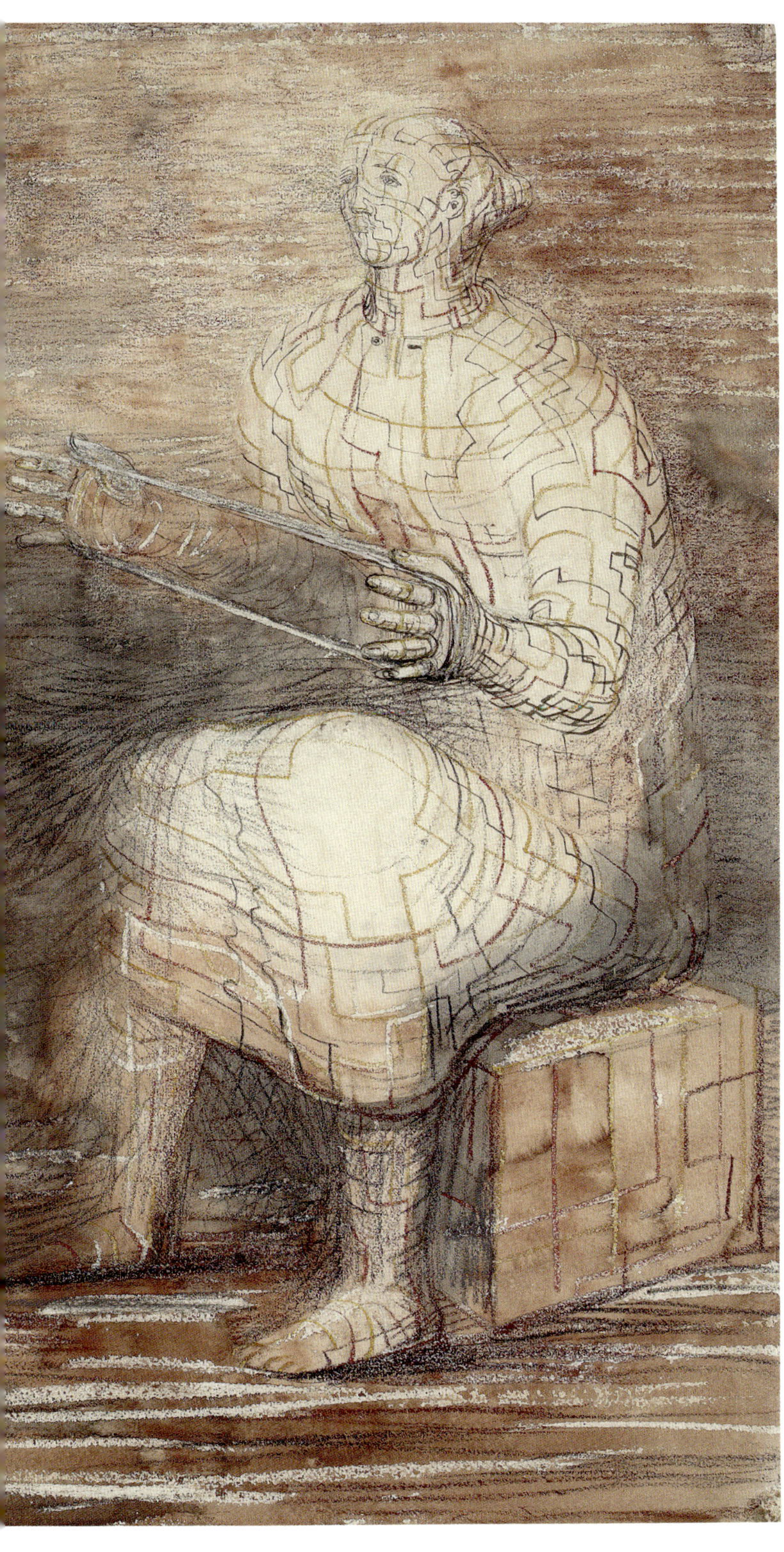

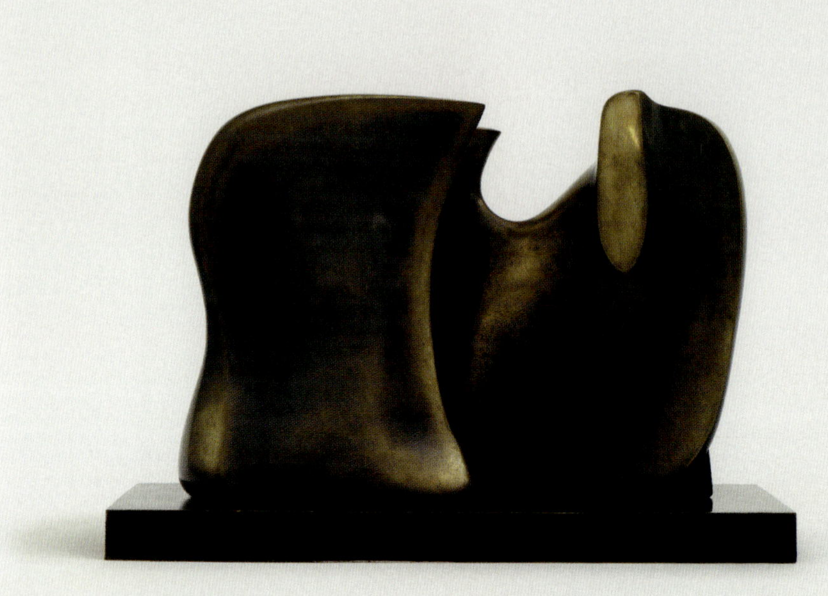

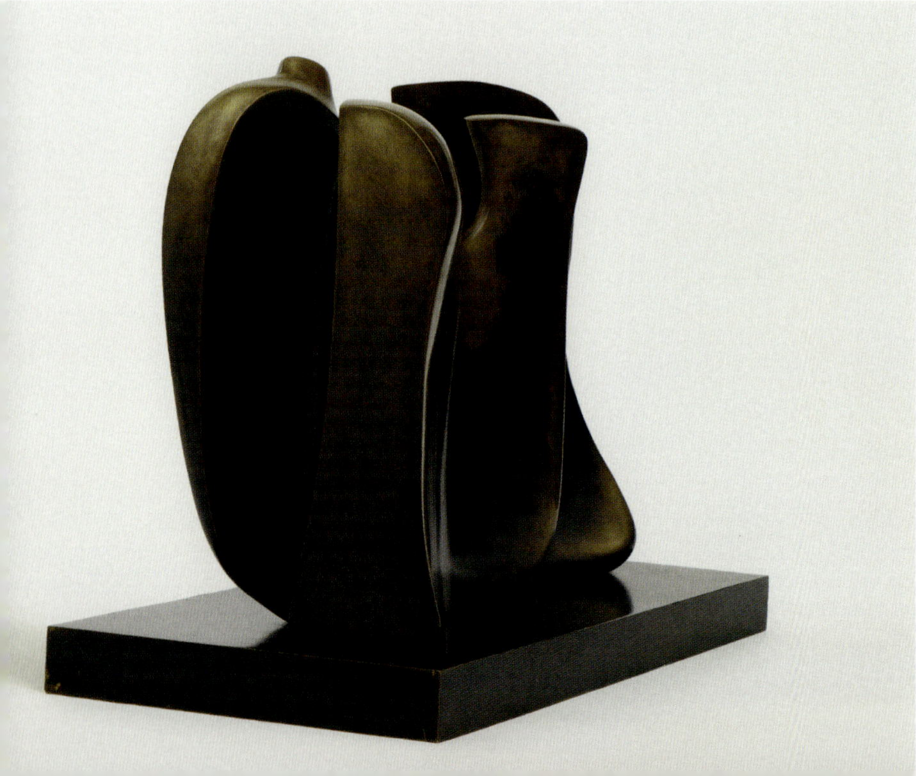

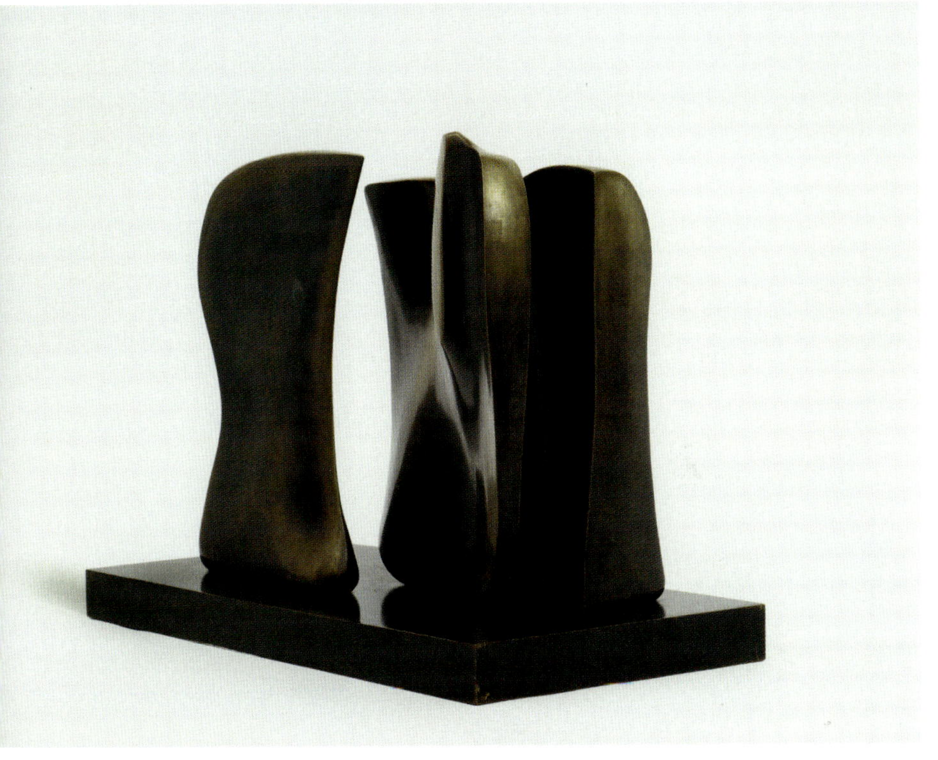

Working Model for Knife Edge Two Piece 1962

Standing Nude, c. 1929

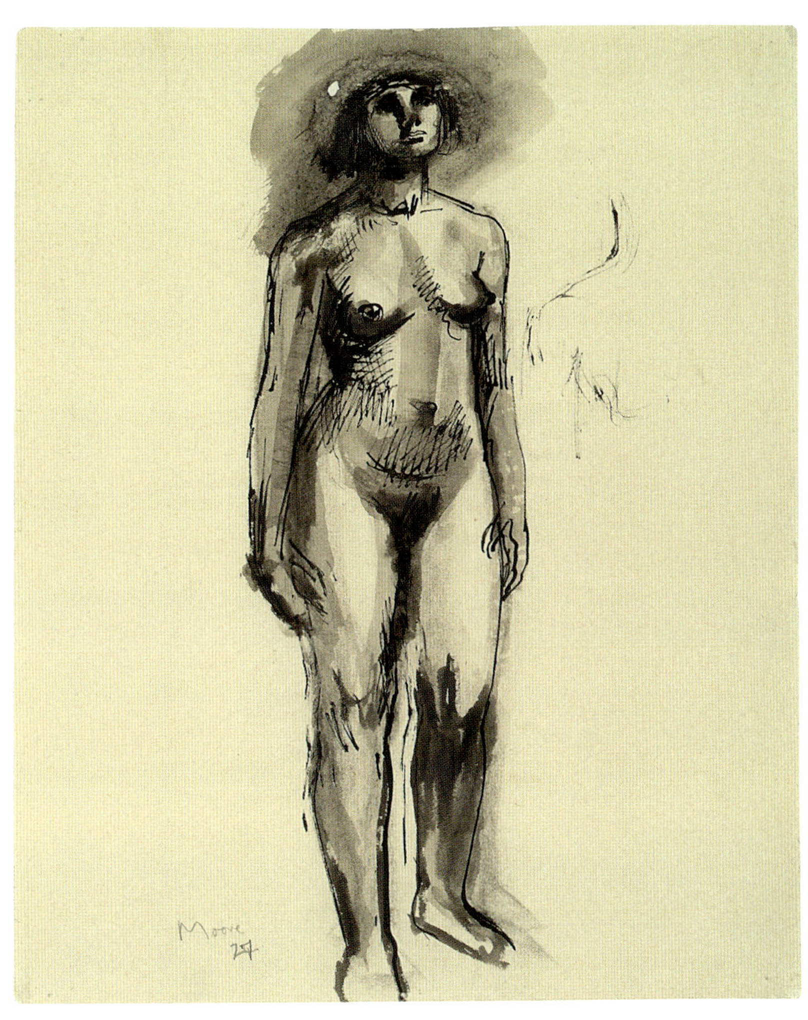

Head: Lines 1955

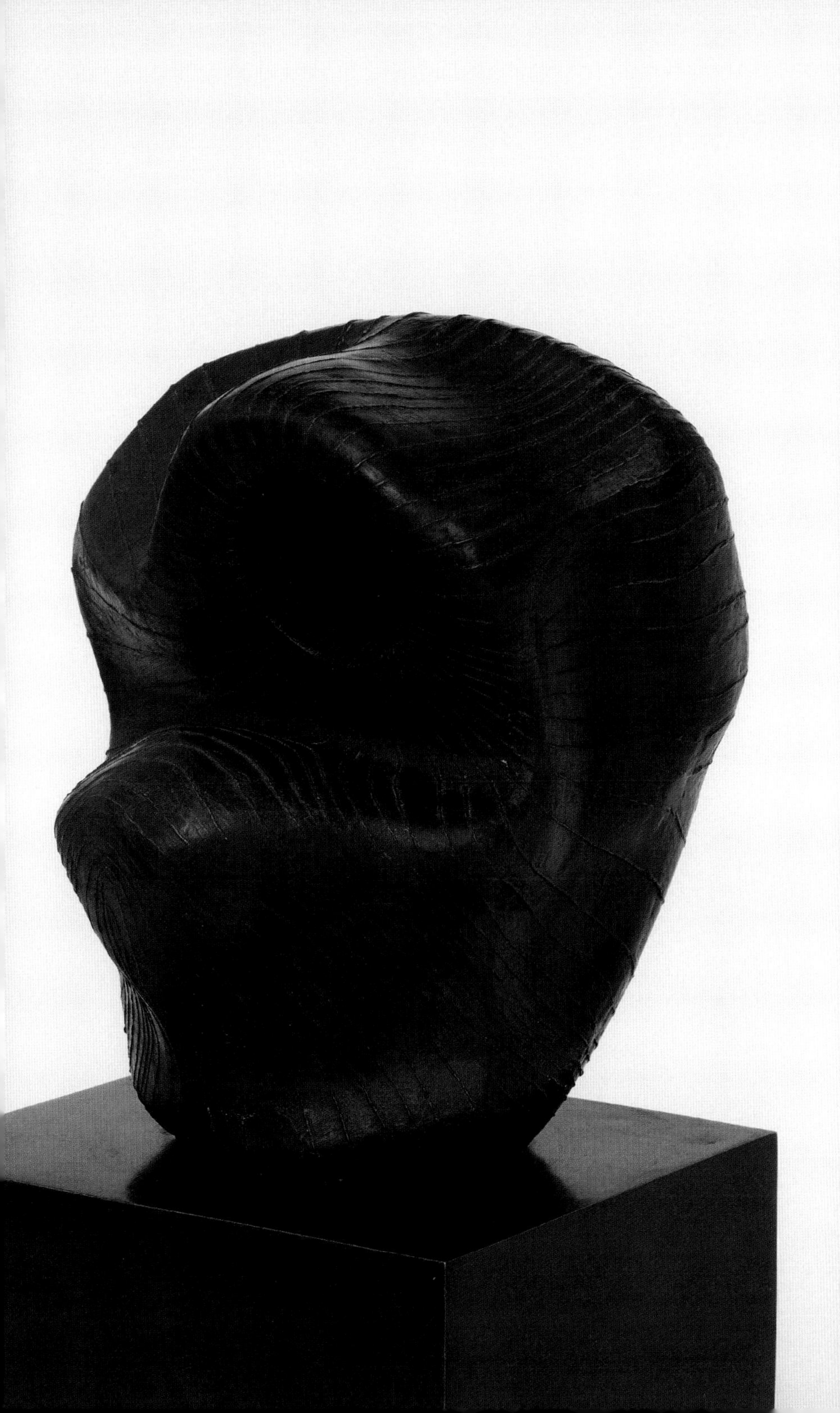

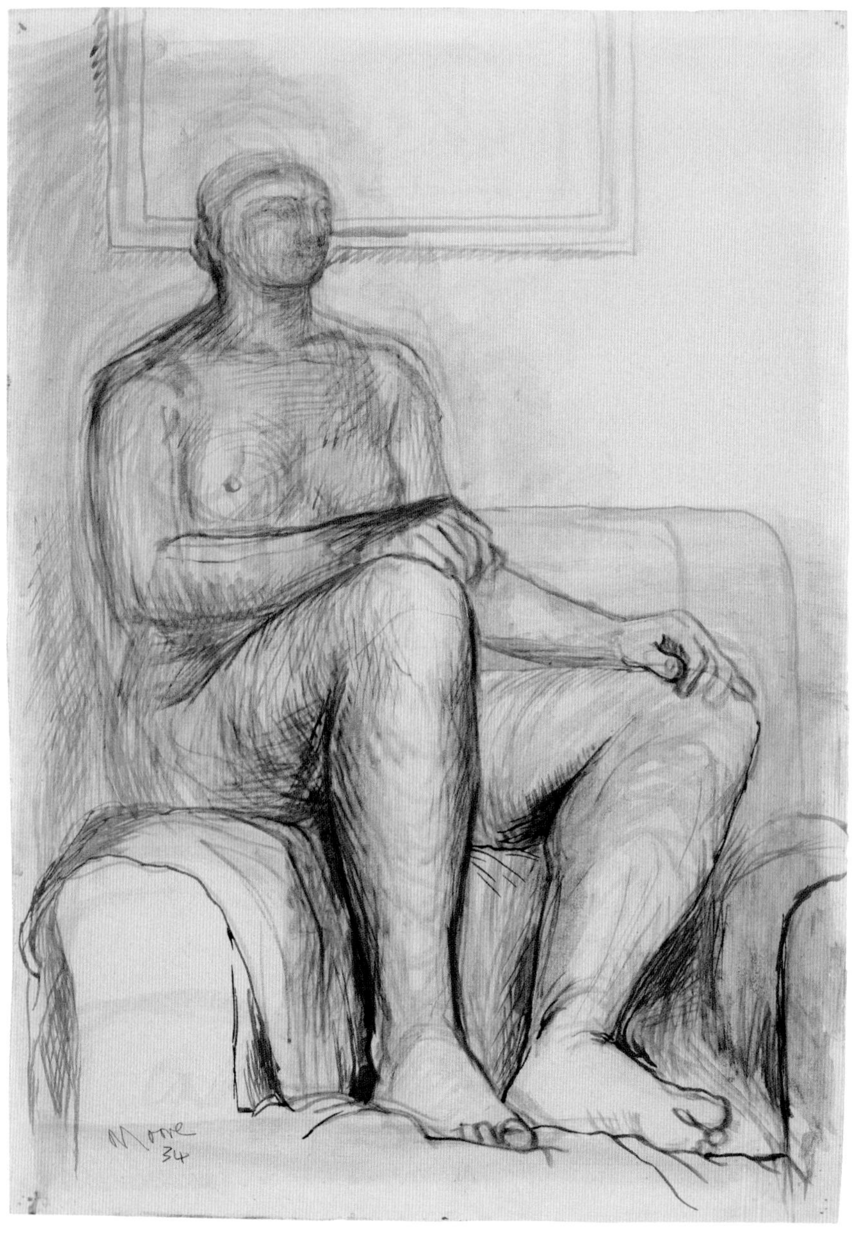

Seated Figure, c. 1933

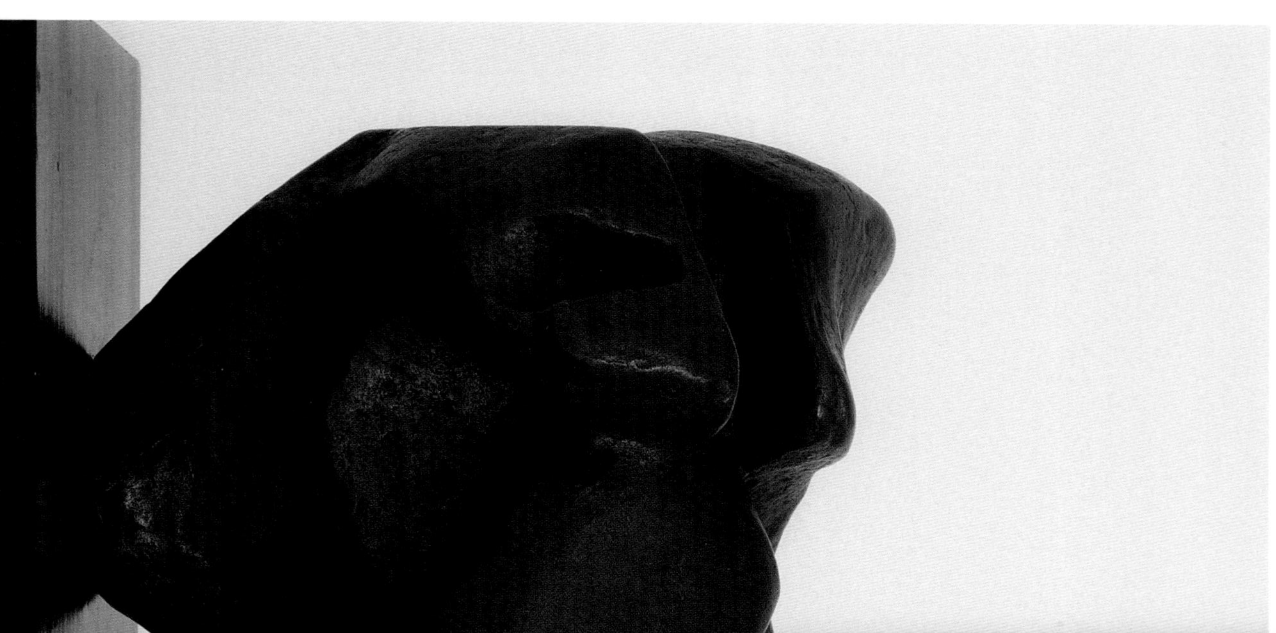

Slow Form: Tortoise 1962

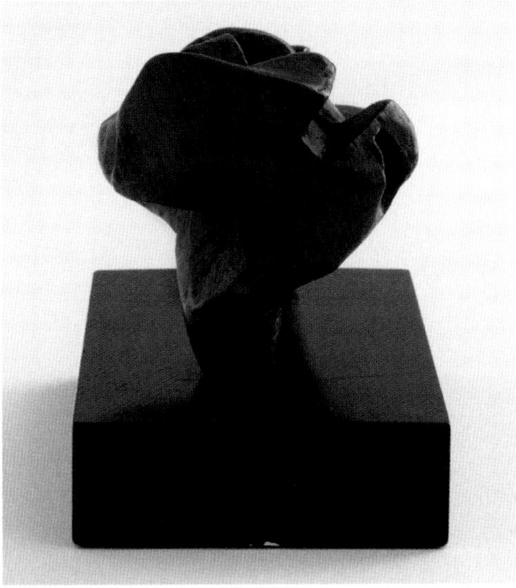

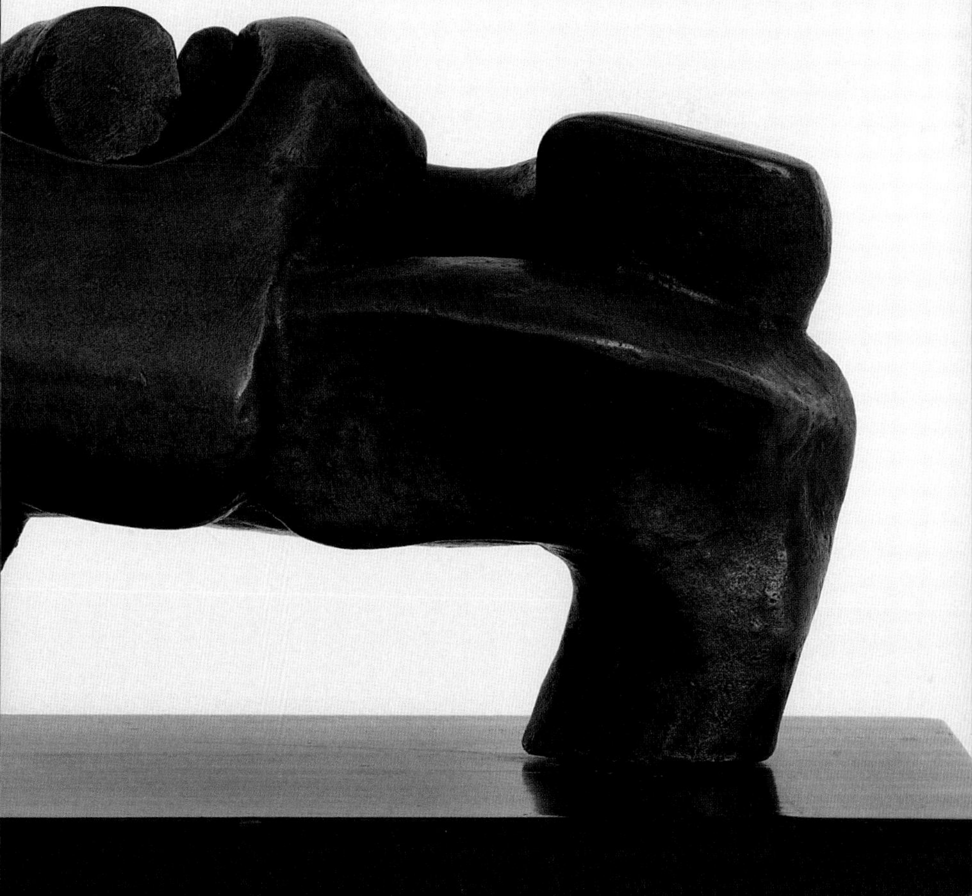

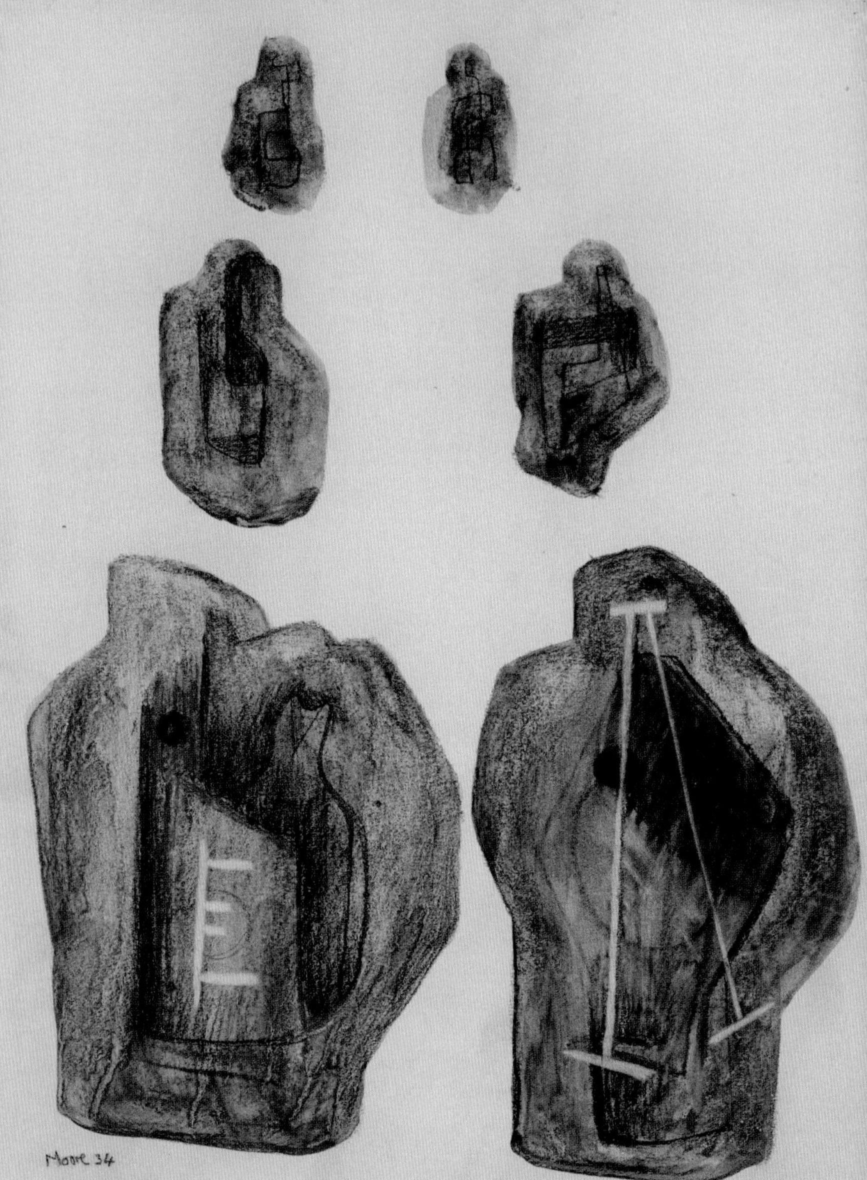

Moore 34

Ideas for Stone Carving, c. 1934

Helmet Head No.3 1960

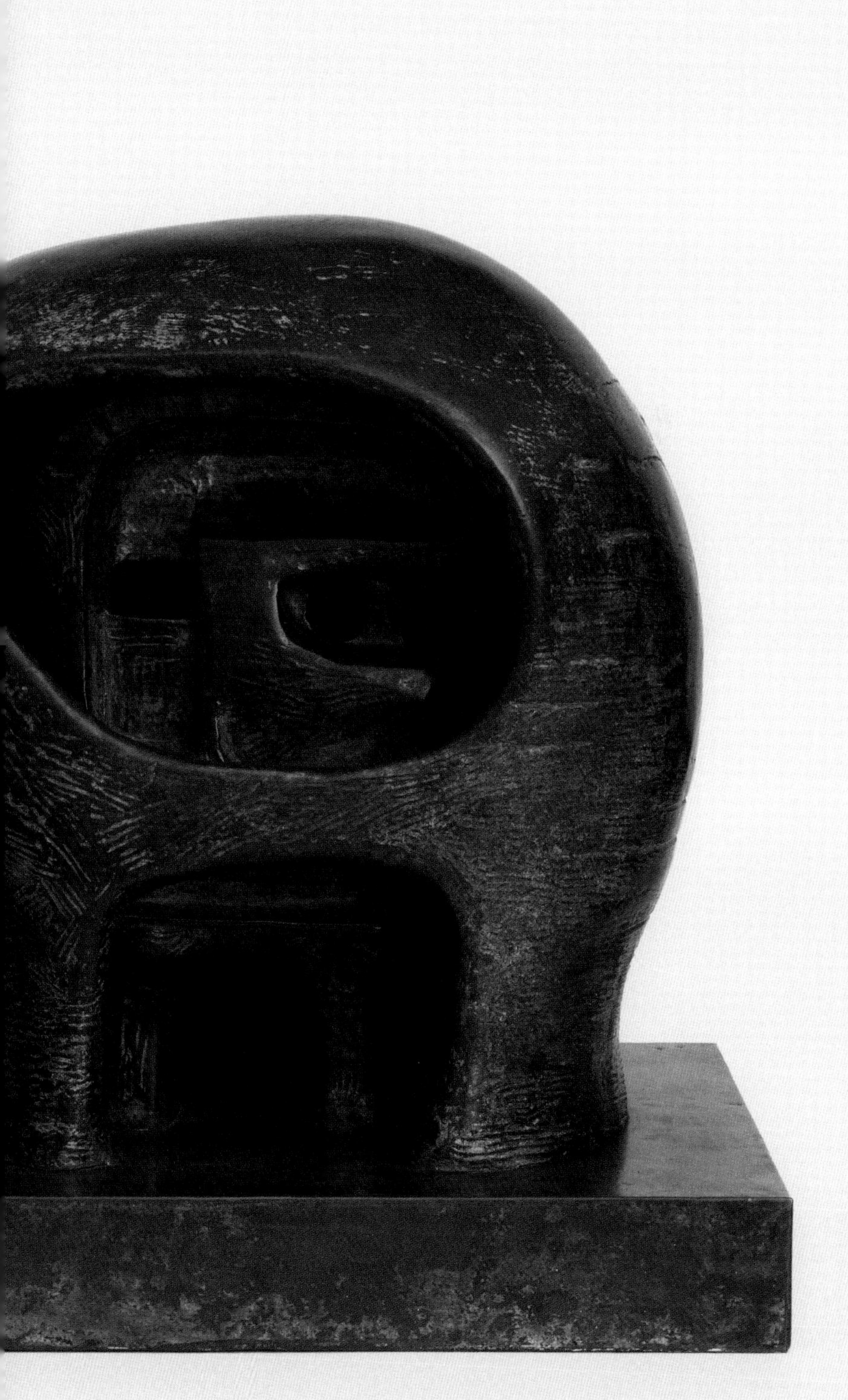

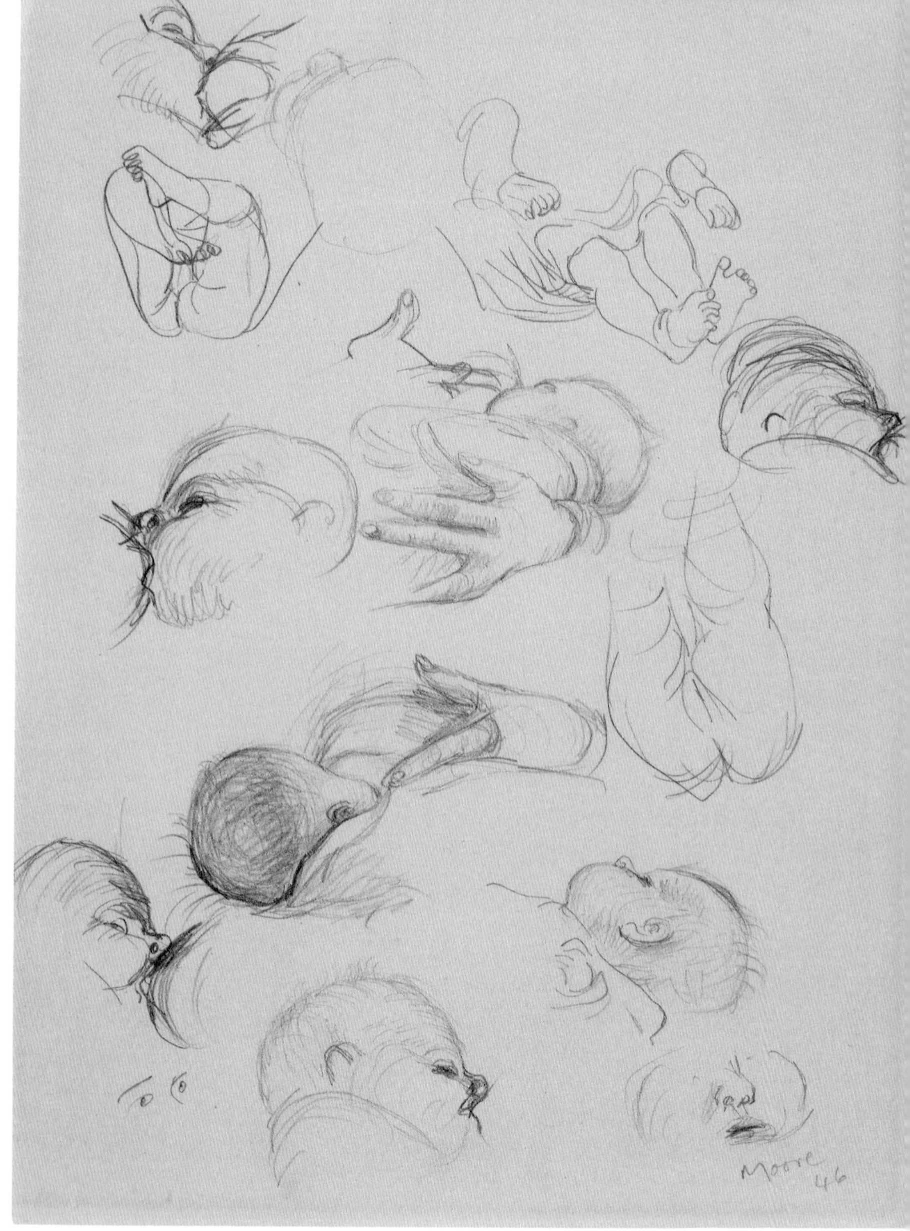

Studies of the Artist's Child 1946

appendices

This list constitutes a complete inventory of Henry Moore works held in the Arts Council Collection (ACC). Both ACC and Henry Moore Foundation (HMF/LH) catalogue numbers are given for reference.

Measurements are given in centimetres, height × width × depth.

list of works

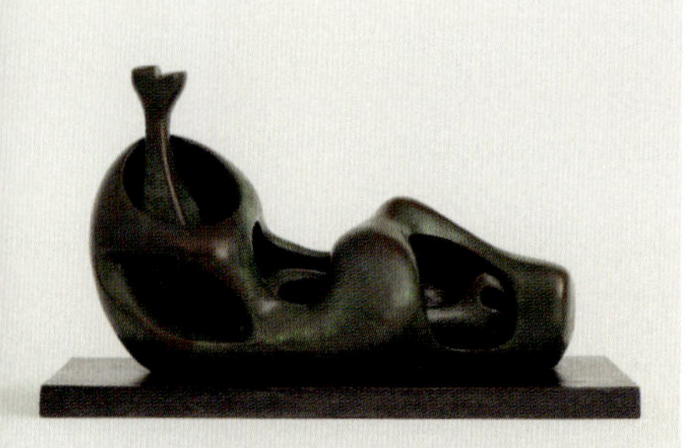

p. 4 (detail), pp. 22–23
Working Model for Reclining Figure: Internal/External Form 1951, cast 1963
Bronze, edition of 8
33 × 52 × 17.1; base: 11.4 × 62.2 × 26
Acquired 1963
ACC7/1963 / LH 298

p. 29
Standing and Reclining Figures 1950
Lithograph on paper,
13 in an edition of 50
29.2 × 24.8
Acquired 1950
PR 283 / CGM 15

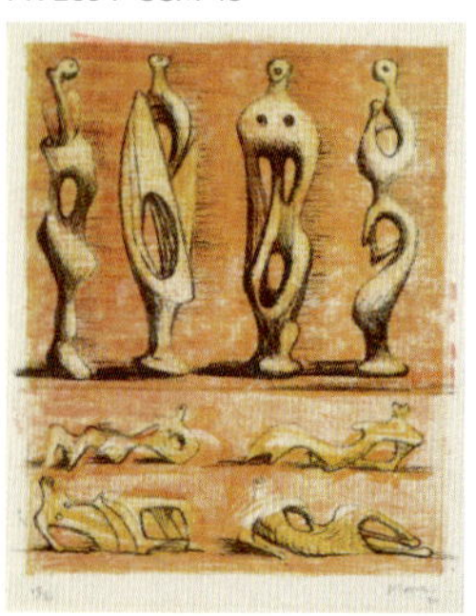

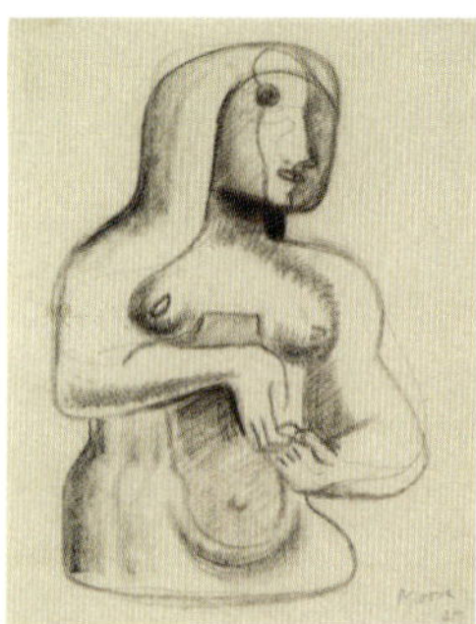

p. 25
Drawing for Figure in Concrete 1929
Pencil, crayon and charcoal on paper
31.4 × 24.2
Acquired 1963
ACC8/1963 / HMF 724

pp. 30–33 (details)
Seated Figure against Curved Wall 1956–57
Bronze, 8 in an edition of 12
56.5 × 91.4 × 53.3
Acquired 1959
AC 485 / LH 422

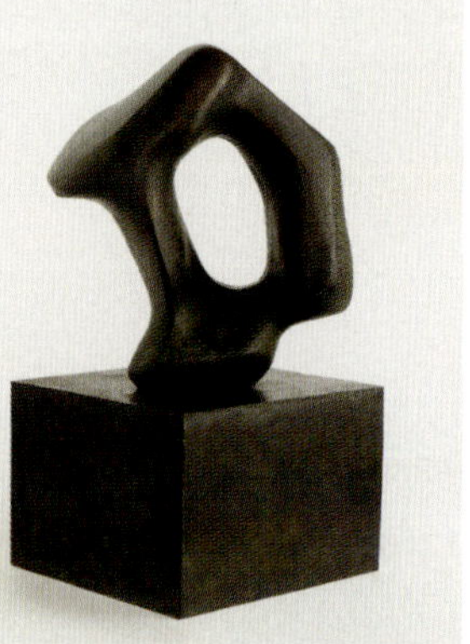

p. 26–27
Sculptural Object 1960
Bronze, 7 in an edition of 10
45.7 × 38.1 × 17.8;
base: 26 × 38.1 × 35.2
Acquired 1963
AC 677 / LH 469

p. 35
Ideas for Sculpture 1932
Brush and ink on paper
36.2 × 26.7
Acquired 1963
AC 685 / HMF 983

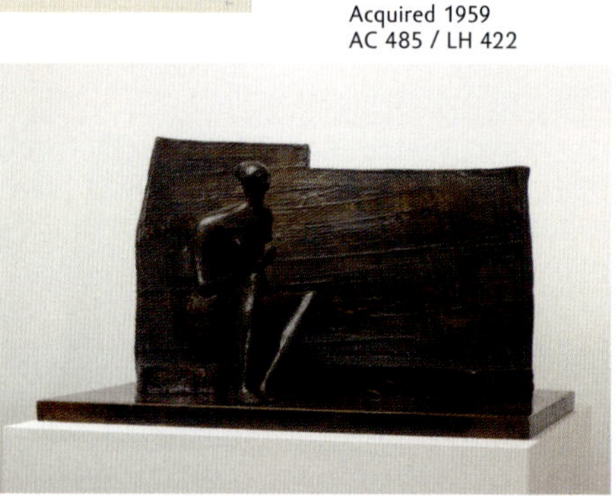

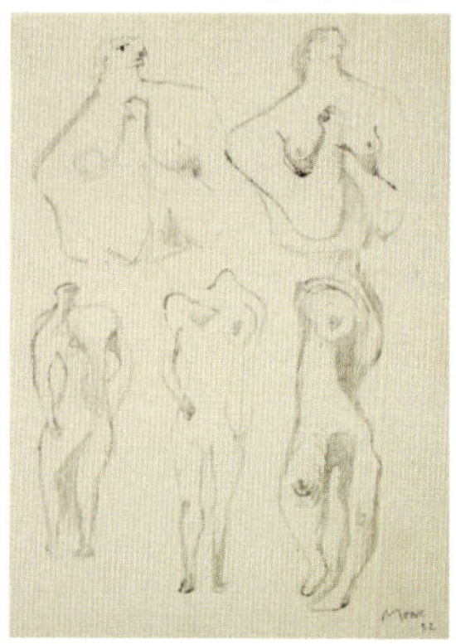

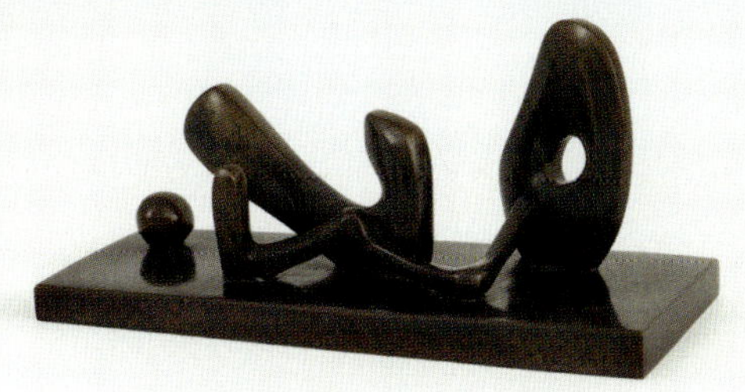

pp. 36–37
Composition 1934, cast 1961
Bronze, edition of 9
23.5 × 52 × 27.9
Acquired 1963
AC 674 / LH 140

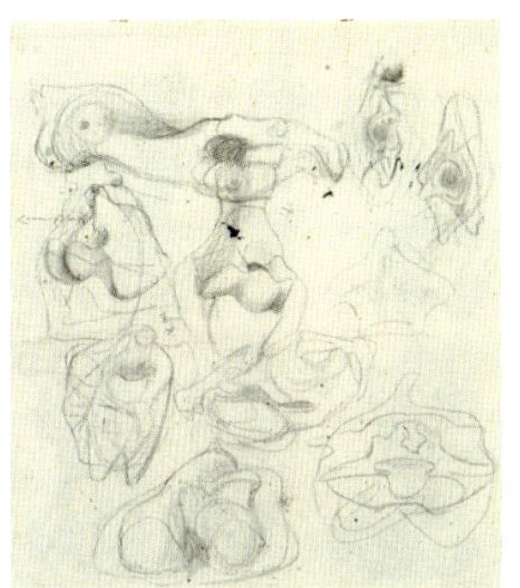
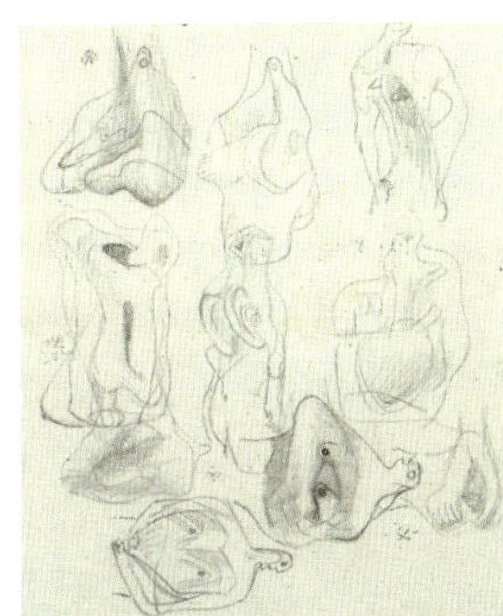

p. 39
*Ideas for Sculpture:
Transformation of Bones* 1932
Pencil on paper
22.9 × 20.3
Acquired 1963
AC 684 b / HMF 970

p. 38
*Ideas for Sculpture:
Transformation of Bones* 1932
Pencil on paper
22.9 × 20.3
Acquired 1963
AC 684 / HMF 969

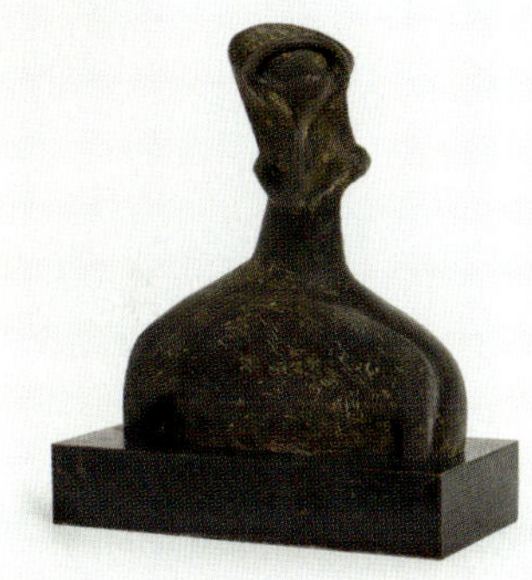

pp. 40–41
Head of a King 1952–53, cast 1962
Bronze, unique cast
58.4 × 48.3 × 20.3
Acquired 1963
ACC5/1963 / LH 351

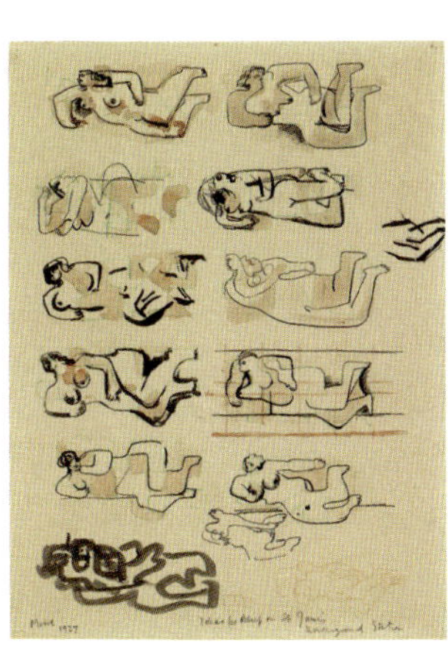

p. 42
Ideas for West Wind Relief,
c. 1927
Watercolour, pen and ink,
and brush and ink on paper
37.5 × 26.7
Acquired 1963
AC 682 / HMF 529

pp. 44–45
*Time/Life Screen:
Working Model* 1952, cast 1964
Bronze, edition of 9
43.2 × 111.1 × 20
Acquired 1964
AC 725 / LH 343

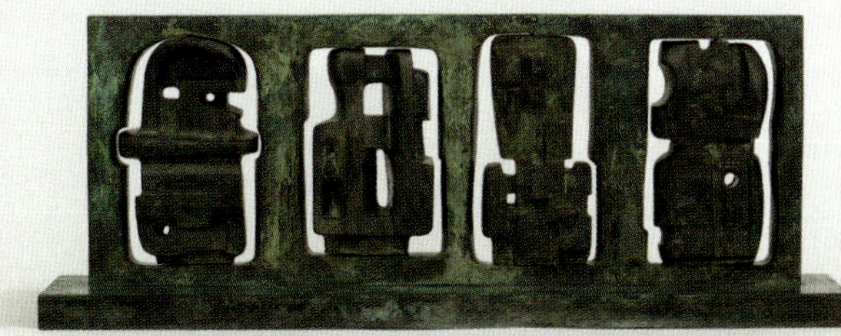

72

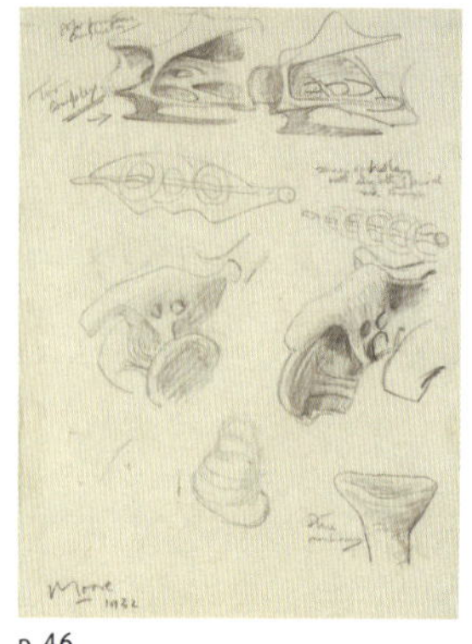

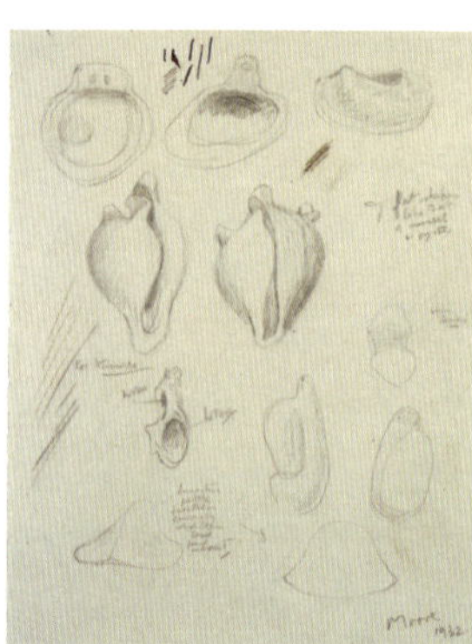

p. 46
*Studies of Bones,
Shell and Mushroom* 1932
Pencil on paper
24.8 × 17.1
Acquired 1963
AC 686 b / HMF 947

pp. 48–49
Stringed Figure 1938, cast 1960
Bronze and string, edition of 12
20.3 × 35.6 × 25.4
Acquired 1963
ACC9/1963 / LH 186b

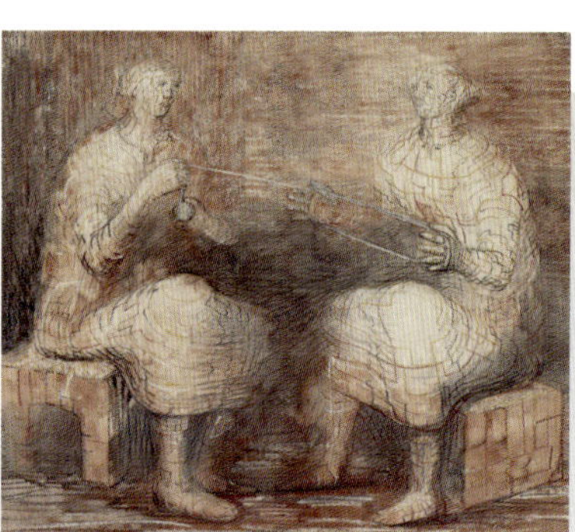

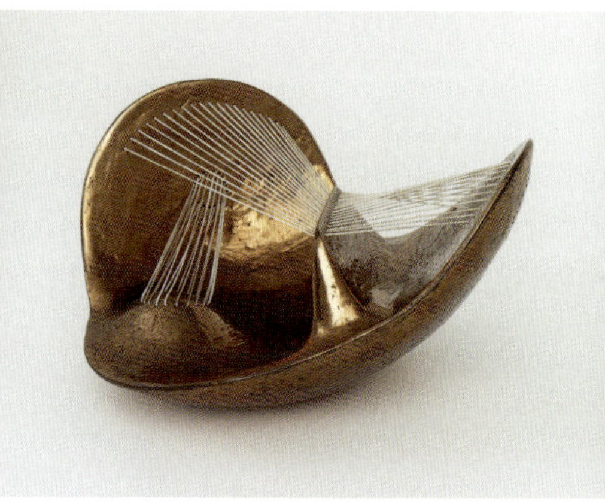

pp. 50–51
Women Winding Wool 1948
Watercolour, pencil, chalk,
wax crayon, and pen and ink
on paper
54.2 × 56.3
Acquired 1948
AC 24 / HMF 2497

p. 55
Standing Nude, c. 1929
Pen and ink and wash
on paper
44.5 × 36.2
Acquired 1955
AC 385 / HMF 712

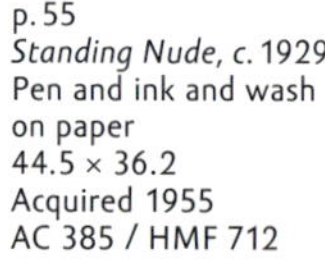

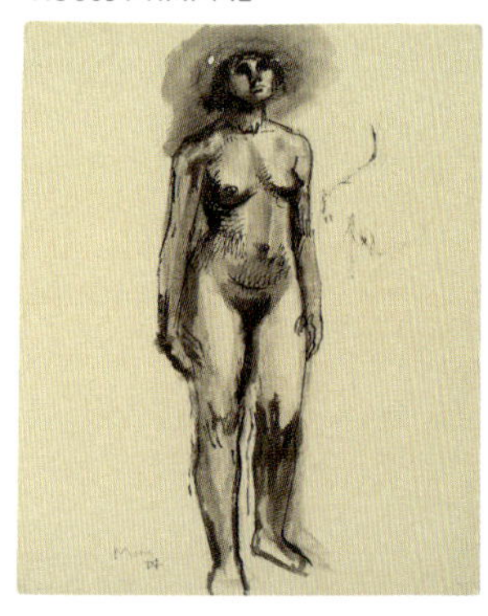

pp. 10–11 (detail), pp. 52–53
Working Model for Knife Edge Two Piece 1962
Bronze, 4 in an edition of 10
44.5 × 58.4 × 22.9
Acquired 1963
ACC6/1963 / LH 504

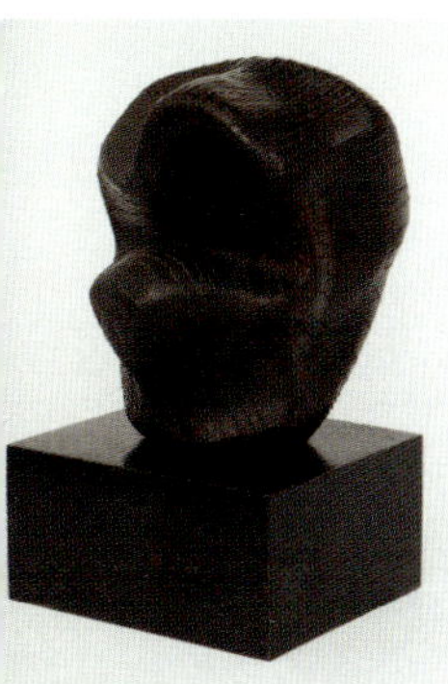

p. 57
Head: Lines 1955
Bronze, 4 in an edition of 6
41.9 × 24.2 × 21;
base: 10.8 × 24.1 × 21
Acquired 1966
AC 840 / LH 397

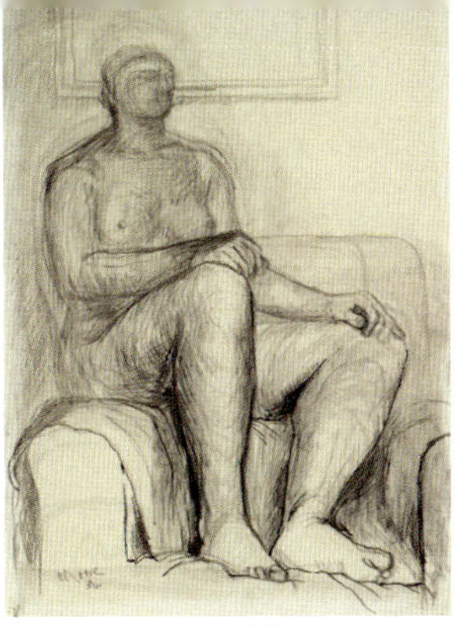

p. 58
Seated Figure, c. 1933
Pencil, wash, and pen and ink on paper
55.5 × 38
Acquired 1948
ACC2/1948 / HMF 1047

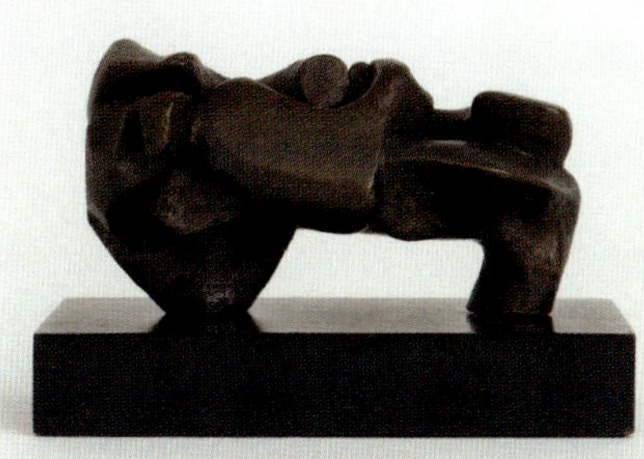

pp. 60–61
Slow Form: Tortoise 1962
Bronze, edition of 9
10.6 × 20.5 × 10
Acquired 1968
ACC10/1968 / LH 502

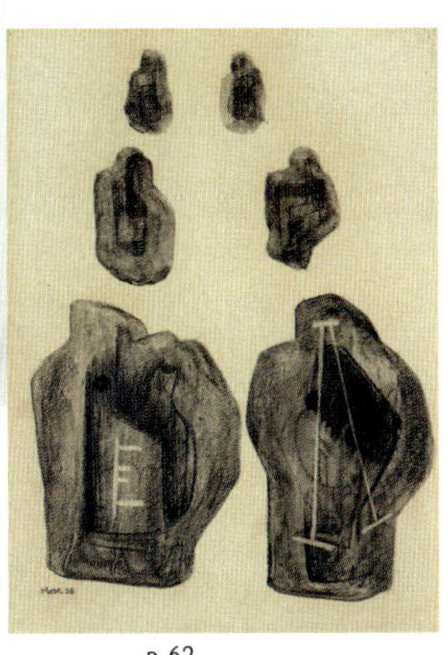

p. 62
Ideas for Stone Carving, c. 1934
Chalk, crayon and wash on paper
49.5 × 36.8
Acquired 1963
AC 687 / HMF 1164

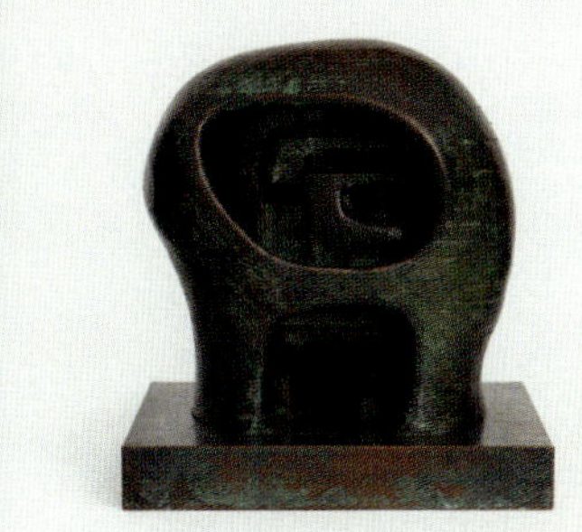

pp. 64–65
Helmet Head No.3 1960
Bronze, 12 in an edition of 14
33 × 33 × 27.9
Acquired 1963
AC 675 / LH 467

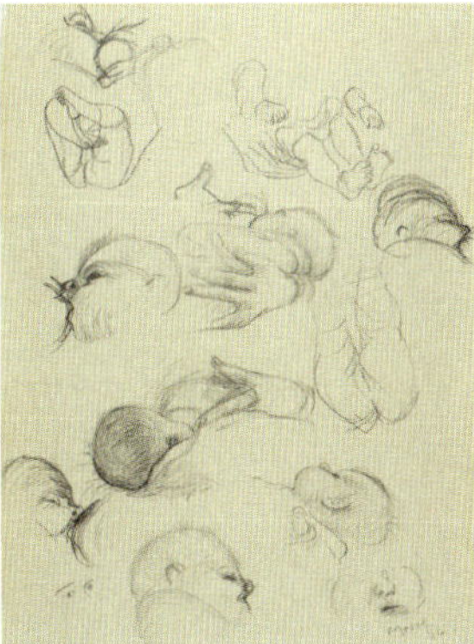

p. 66
Studies of the Artist's Child 1946
Pencil on paper
38.1 × 27.9
Acquired 1954
AC 298 / HMF 2359

3 BRITISH ARTISTS HENRY MOORE JOHN PIPER GRAHAM SUTHERLAND EXHIBITION

CATALOGUE

ORGANISED FOR C.E.M.A. BY THE
BRITISH INSTITUTE OF ADULT EDUCATION
29 TAVISTOCK SQUARE LONDON WCI

3 D

a

timeline

1898

— Henry Moore born 30 July at Castleford, Yorkshire.

1910

— Wins scholarship to Castleford Secondary School to train as a teacher, going on to gain a post as a student teacher in his old school, Temple Street Elementary, in 1916.

1917–19

— Serves as Private in 15th Battalion, London Regiment, Civil Service Rifles. After being gassed at the Battle of Cambrai, he is invalided back to England, serving for the remainder of the war as a physical training instructor.

1919

— Becomes the first student of sculpture at Leeds School of Art on an ex-serviceman's education grant. Meets fellow art student Barbara Hepworth.

1921

— Wins a scholarship to study at Royal College of Art, London. After graduation, he is appointed as a sculpture instructor at the College, teaching there until 1931. It was also at Royal College of Art that he met his future wife, painting student Irina Radetsky.

1925

— Visits Paris, Rome, Florence, Venice and Ravenna on a travelling scholarship.

1928

— First public commission, for a relief on London Underground Railway headquarters, St James's Street (see *Ideas for West Wind Relief*, *c.* 1927, p. 42).

1932

— Becomes the first Head of Sculpture in a new department at Chelsea School of Art.

1933

— Kenneth Clark appointed Director of National Gallery. Clark was an important advocate of Moore's work and a founding member of the Arts Council of Great Britain (ACGB) board, serving as its Chairman between 1955 and 1960. Clark was formative in the programming of the 1951 Festival of Britain and a Chairman of the War Artists Advisory Committee, commissioning work by Moore in both capacities.

1934

— First monograph on the artist, *Henry Moore* by Herbert Read, is published. Read will go on to serve on the ACGB Art Panel from 1947–1953.

1936

— Moore shows works at the *International Surrealist Exhibition* in London, working with Roland Penrose on the organising committee.

1937

— Roland Penrose buys *Mother and Child* (1936) sculpture from Moore and displays the work in his front garden in Hampstead, London. Local residents and press campaign for it to be removed, describing it as 'deformities in stone'

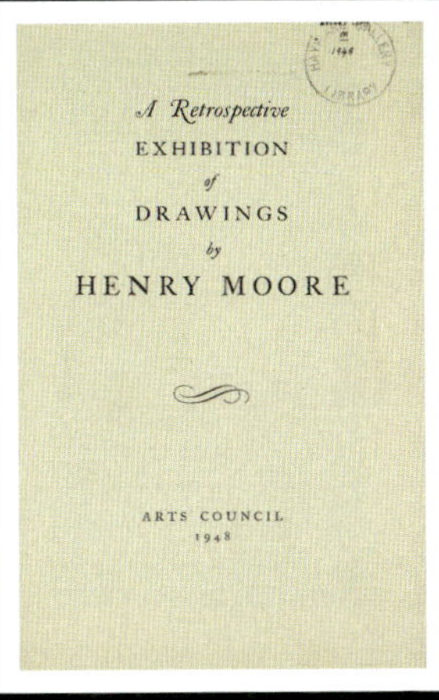

b

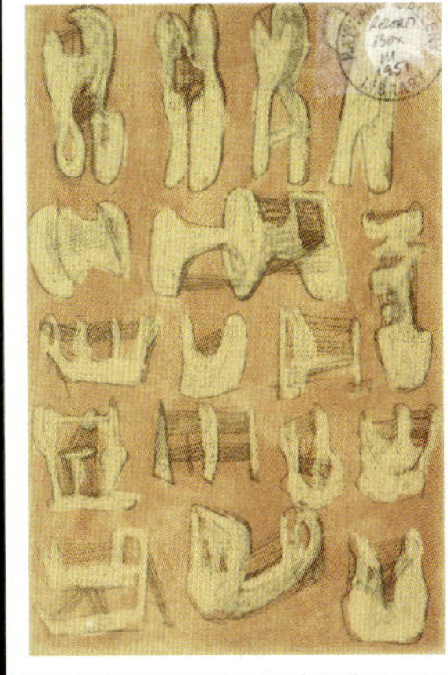

c

1940
— Moore's Hampstead studio is hit by shrapnel, instigating his move to Perry Green, Much Hadham.
— The Council for the Encouragement of Music and Arts (CEMA) is established to promote British cultural activity, chaired by Lord De La Warr, President of the Board of Education. Kenneth Clark is a founding board member, with Moore, who serves on the CEMA art panel between 1942 and 1944.

1941
— *3 British Artists: Moore, Piper, Sutherland* exhibition at the Leeds Country House Museum at Temple Newsam. The exhibition is organised for CEMA by the British Institute of Adult Education (BIAE), London (catalogue, fig. a).

1942
— Philip James is appointed Director of Art at CEMA.

1945
— Critic and curator David Sylvester writes a review of critic Herbert Read's *Henry Moore: Sculpture and Drawing* in the *Tribune* magazine. Moore contacts Sylvester as a result and they go on to become life-long friends and colleagues. Sylvester was later to sit on the Art Panel at ACGB (1961–75) and presented Moore's work for purchase.

1945
— Arts Council of Great Britain (ACGB) is established, taking ownership of CEMA collection (which becomes the Arts Council Collection) and developing a touring programme. Moore is appointed a member of the Art Panel, advising the Council on matters of policy and development in the visual arts—a position he holds until 1951.

1946
— The ACGB first *Sculpture in the Home* exhibition features Moore's small sculptures in domestic settings, positioning the home as a new context for modern art. His work will be shown in all four exhibitions in this series (1953 catalogue, fig. e).

1948
— The Collection purchases two drawings by Moore: *Seated Figure, c.* 1933 (p. 58) and *Women Winding Wool 1948* (pp. 50–51).
— *A Retrospective Exhibition of Drawings by Henry Moore*, organised by the ACGB (catalogue, fig. b).

1951
— Moore retrospective held at Tate, arranged by ACGB for the Festival of Britain, and curated by David Sylvester: *Sculpture and Drawings by Henry Moore* (catalogues, figs c & d).
— ACGB commission large bronze *Reclining Figure*, which is placed near the main entrance to the South Bank site for the Festival of Britain.

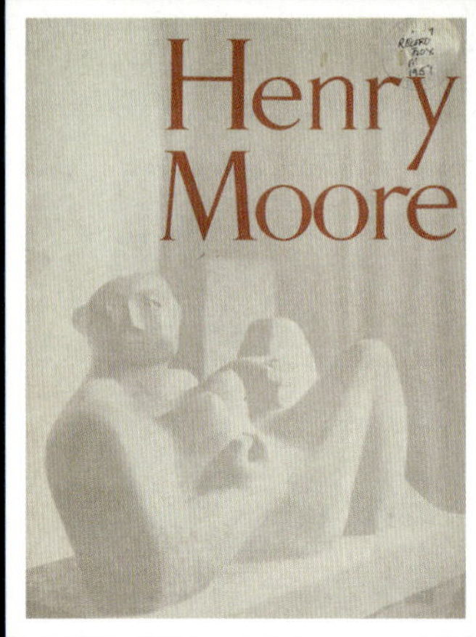

d

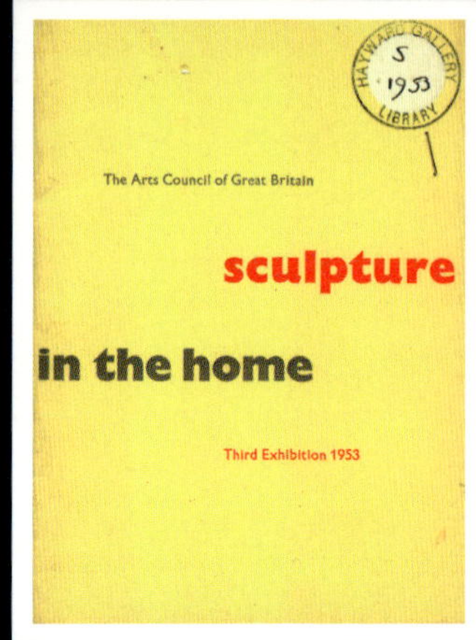

e

1954

— *Studies of the Artist's Child* 1946 (p. 66) acquired by the Collection on 23 February.

1955

— *Standing Nude, c.*1929 (p. 55) acquired by the Collection on 9 December.
— Moore undertakes prestigious *Reclining Figure* commission for the UNESCO building in Paris (see *Working Model for Reclining Figure: Internal/External Form* 1951, cast 1963, pp. 22–23).
— Moore is reappointed to the Art Panel of the ACGB, serving until 1960.

1958

— Gabriel White, previously Assistant Director of Art at ACGB, becomes Director—a position he will hold until 1970.

1959

— *Seated Figure against Curved Wall* 1956–57 (pp. 30–33) acquired by the Collection 26 January.

1960

— Moore recommends *Woman Flower* (1959), the work of his former assistant, artist Philip King, for acquisition by ACGB (members of the Art Panel often also acted as purchasers for the Collection).
— Future Director of Henry Moore Foundation Alan Bowness and William Coldstream both sat on the Art Panel with Moore in this year, working together closely to oversee acquisitions for the Collection.

1961

— David Sylvester invited to join the Art Panel of ACGB, advising on policy.

1962

— From 17 February to 5 May, an exhibition of Moore's sculpture and drawings, organised by ACGB, tours UK venues (poster, fig. f).
— In summer, Gabriel White and Lord Cottesloe (Chairman of ACGB and the Southbank board) visit Moore's studio at Perry Green to discuss future acquisition of sculptures and drawings.

1963

— Penrose and Sylvester, among others, sit on the Art Panel at the time of a significant Moore purchase: eight drawings and eight sculptures by Moore are acquired, as listed below (please see list of works for page nos, acquisition dates are listed where known). A touring exhibition is quickly organised to show the new acquisitions at regional galleries across the UK.

Drawings:

Drawing for Figure in Concrete 1929 (acquired 10 May, p. 25)
Ideas for Sculpture 1932 (acq. 10 May, p. 35)
Ideas for Sculpture: Transformation of Bones 1932 (p. 38)
Ideas for Sculpture: Transformation of Bones 1932 (p. 39)
Ideas for Stone Carving 1934 (acq. 10 May, p. 62)
*Ideas for West Wind Relief, c.*1927 (p. 42)
Studies of Bones, Shell and Mushroom 1932 (p. 46)
Studies of Shells and Pebbles 1932 (p. 47)

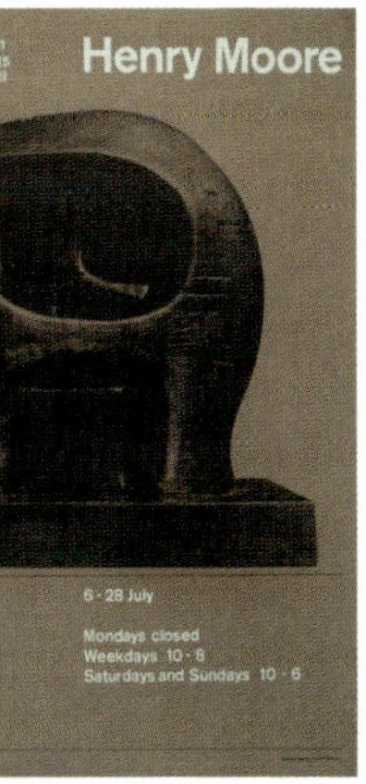

f

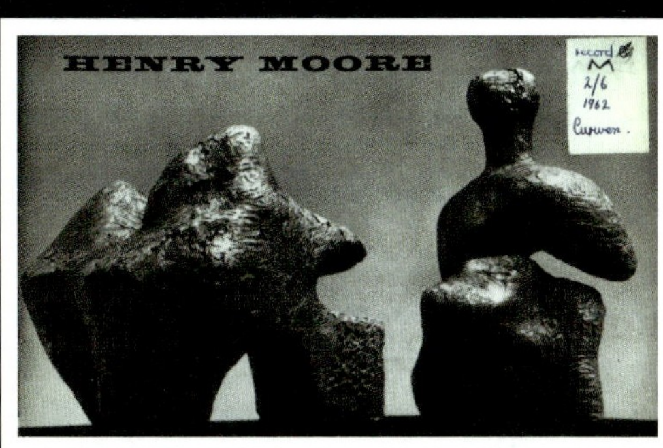

g

Sculptures:
  Composition 1934, cast 1961
  (acq. 10 May, pp. 36–37)
  Head of a King 1952–53, cast
  1962 (pp. 40–41)
  Helmet Head No.3 1960
  (acq. 10 May, pp. 64–65)
  Sculptural Object 1960
  (acq. 10 May, pp. 26–27)
  Stringed Figure 1938, cast 1960
  (pp. 48–49)
  *Time/Life Screen: Working
  Model* 1952, plaster cast 1963
  (pp. 44–45)
  *Working Model for Knife Edge
  Two Piece* 1962 (acq. 10 May,
  pp. 52–53)
  *Working Model for Reclining
  Figure: Internal/ External
  Form* 1951, cast 1963

— David Sylvester recommends
Slow Form: Tortoise 1962 (pp. 60–61)
for acquisition. This is the last Moore
work to enter the Collection.

1970
— Robin Campbell succeeds Gabriel
White as Director of Art at ACGB.

1972
— The Henry Moore Trust is set up
to safeguard the artist's legacy
and estate.

1975
— Joanna Drew succeeds Robin Campbell
at ACGB as Director of Art.

1977
— The Henry Moore Foundation is
established at Perry Green,

Andrew Causey,
The Drawings of Henry Moore,
Lund Humphries, London, 2010.

Anita Feldman and Malcolm Woodward,
Henry Moore: Plasters,
Royal Academy of Arts, London, 2011.

David Mitchinson,
Celebrating Moore:
Works from the Collection of
The Henry Moore Foundation,
Lund Humphries, London, 2006.

David Mitchinson,
Henry Moore: Prints and Portfolios,
Patrick Cramer, Geneva, 2010.

David Mitchinson et al.,
Hoglands: The Home of Henry and Irina Moore,
Lund Humphries, London, 2007.

Henry Moore at Perry Green,
Scala, London, 2011.

Chris Stephens,
Henry Moore,
Tate Publishing, London, 2010.

Alan Wilkinson (ed.),
Henry Moore: Writings and Conversations,
Documents of Twentieth-Century Art,
University of California Press, Berkeley, CA, 2002.

further reading

All artwork photography courtesy
Arts Council Collection, Southbank Centre,
London. Reproduced by permission of
The Henry Moore Foundation.
Artwork photography: Anna Arca pp. 4–5,
10–11, 22–23, 26–27, 30–33, 36–37,
40–41, 44–45, 48–49, 52–53, 57, 60–61,
64–65 and corresponding images 70–73.
Archival photography courtesy Hayward
Library and Archive, Southbank Centre,
London pp. 75l, 75r, 76l, 76r, 77r.
Archival photography courtesy The Henry
Moore Foundation pp. 13, 15, 16, 19, 77l.
© image: Imperial War Museum (GP/ 46/
24/13. Item 31) p. 74.

A catalogue record for this book is available
from the British Library

ISBN: 978 1 85332 302 7

This catalogue is not intended to be used
for authentication or related purposes.
The Southbank Board Limited accepts no
liability for any errors or omissions that the
catalogue may inadvertently contain.

Distributed in North America,
Central America and South America by
D.A.P. / Distributed Art Publishers, Inc.,
155 Sixth Avenue, 2nd Floor, New York,
NY 10013
tel: +212 627 1999
fax: +212 627 9484
www.artbook.com

Distributed in the UK and Europe,
by Cornerhouse Publications
70 Oxford Street, Manchester M1 5NH
tel: +44 (0)161 200 1503
fax: +44 (0)161 200 1504
www.cornerhouse.org/books

Published on the occasion of the exhibition
Henry Moore and the Arts Council Collection

Canterbury Royal Museum and Art Gallery
8 September – 28 October 2012

Victoria Art Gallery, Bath
3 April – 23 June 2013

The Hunt Museum, Limerick
24 August – 3 November 2013

The Lightbox, Woking
23 November 2013 – 12 January 2014

Exhibition organised by Jill Constantine
and Natalie Rudd with Lizzie Simpson,
Laura Robinson and Helen Kaplinsky.

This exhibition has been made possible
by the provision of insurance through the
Government Indemnity Scheme. The Arts
Council Collection would like to thank
HM Government for providing Government
Indemnity and the Department for Culture,
Media and Sport and Arts Council England
for arranging the indemnity.

Published by Hayward Publishing
Southbank Centre
Belvedere Road
London, SE1 8XX, UK
www.southbankcentre.co.uk

Art Publisher: Nadine Monem
Staff Editor: Faye Robson
Sales Manager: Deborah Power
Catalogue designed by Pony Ltd.,
www.ponybox.co.uk
Colour management by Dexter Pre-Media
Printed in Italy by Graphicom